Debt Free, Cashed Up AND Laughing

Debt Free, Cashed Up and Laughing

THE CHEAPSKATES WAY TO LIVING THE GOOD LIFE

Cath Armstrong & Lea-Anne Brighton

ABC
Books

The ABC 'Wave' device is a trademark of the Australian Broadcasting Corporation and is used under licence by HarperCollins*Publishers* Australia.

This edition first published in 2007 by ABC Books for
the Australian Broadcasting Corporation.
Reprinted by HarperCollins*Publishers* Australia Pty Limited
ABN 36 009 913 517
harpercollins.com.au

HarperCollins*Publishers*
Level 13, 201 Elizabeth Street, Sydney, NSW 2000, Australia
31 View Road, Glenfield, Auckland 0627, New Zealand
A 53, Sector 57, Noida, UP, India
77–85 Fulham Palace Road, London W6 8JB, United Kingdom
2 Bloor Street East, 20th floor, Toronto, Ontario M4W 1A8, Canada
10 East 53rd Street, New York NY 10022, USA

National Library of Australia Cataloguing-in-Publication entry
   Armstrong, Cath.
   Debt free, cashed up and laughing : the cheapskates way to
   living the good life.
   Bibliography.
   Includes index.
   ISBN 978 0 7333 2112 2.
   1. Finance, Personal. 2. Saving and investment.
   I. Brighton, Lea-Anne. II. Australian Broadcasting Corporation.
   III. Title.
332.024

Cover and text designs by Nanette Backhouse / SASO content and design
Typeset by Kirby Jones

Contents

Part 3: Cheapskate Success Stories

Appendixes

Index

Introduction

Welcome to the Cheapskate Way to Live

Let us share a little with you about becoming a Cheapskate. The Cheapskate way to live is all about being debt-free and living comfortably within your means. Our practical strategies have helped thousands of people adjust their habits so that they can pay off credit cards and debts and minimise loans and mortgages. But the most important component to being a Cheapskate is to have fun while you are saving money.

You might be:

- Struggling with credit card debt
- Spending hundreds of dollars each month on clothes and shoes
- Living a lifestyle that you can't afford
- Finding it tough with interest rates on the rise
- Paying ridiculously high repayments on loans and going backwards
- Feeling as though you can't get ahead
- Wanting to stop work and have children
- Dreaming of taking the children on holiday
- Needing a new car
- Wanting to sleep at night without worrying
- Needing to stop fighting with your partner over money
- Wanting the freedom to make choices

We invite you to take a look at some of the useful ways that you can save money. Being a Cheapskate does not mean that you are miserly or stingy with your time, money or family. In fact, it is quite the opposite. People who follow the Cheapskate way of life enjoy an abundance and are happy to share. The people we know who are Cheapskates share these common traits:

Quality not quantity
The Cheapskate way is to save, not spend money. Cheapskates buy quality not quantity and want good value for money rather than a cheap price. A Cheapskate recognises the true value in saving to get exactly what they want.

Avoid unnecessary spending
Cheapskates buy what they need, when they need it and when they can afford it.

Not afraid to save up
Cheapskates shop around to get the most from every dollar. A Cheapskate will spend money; however, they will look for the best value for their dollar. In most cases this means saving to get something that is of good quality, that will last a long time and is exactly what they want, rather than buying a cheap version now.

Time is valuable
Cheapskates recognise the value of time and plan accordingly. Cheapskates don't want to waste time in long queues or shop at busy times; they want to use that time to spend with family or friends, so they plan ahead and maximise their efficiency in all aspects of life.

Choices

Cheapskates know what they are doing and this provides them with an enormous number of options. They are not living week-to-week getting caught out all the time and feeling stressed. Sure, there are always challenges, but they plan for the unexpected and, as a result, have the luxury of choice.

An Invitation to be a Cheapskate

We have been Cheapskates for many years now and it has given us the money to provide our families with the quality of life that brings about the freedom to do what we want. Here are some of the things that we value and have achieved by being Cheapskates:

Family holidays

Being Cheapskates means that we holiday and have fun without debt, so there are no credit cards for us to repay. We save and pay for the trip as we go. It takes the stress and strain away and we all enjoy the time we spend together. Some wonderful family holidays we've enjoyed include: camping at the beach for two weeks at Christmas; going to a lodge in the snowfields and camping in the bush. We are about to embark on an overseas holiday!

Education

Our children attend private schools because we always wanted them to have the best education that was available. We know that we have made sacrifices; however, it has been worth it to see the children excel at school.

Hobbies and interests

Living the Cheapskate way we have been able to pursue the different hobbies and interests that lead to a rich and full life: my husband is a keen train buff with thousands of dollars of toys, I love crafts and scrapbooking and the children are busy and engaged in activities, sports and various hobbies.

Tasty food

It seems that it is becoming more and more popular to provide meals from a can, bottle or packet. Each week millions of meals are purchased from restaurants, takeaway shops and fast food outlets. These meals cost more. Cheapskates learn to cook meals that are tasty, nutritious and filling. The family enjoy the taste more and it saves us thousands of dollars each year. Sure, we go out occasionally; however, most nights we eat as a family at the dinner table. Our children are fit and healthy and we spend time talking and enjoying each other's company.

Can You Live the Cheapskate Way?

While many believe that some people are born Cheapskates, the truth is that being a Cheapskate can be learned.

Here is a quick quiz to see if you are or can become a Cheapskate. Do you:

- Want to be debt free?
- Like saving money when you shop?
- Love a bargain?
- Buy what you need (don't shop for retail therapy)?
- Hate paying high interest rates?

- Want to have the money for a fun retirement?
- Choose to be financially secure?
- Want to have a great lifestyle?

  Here are some other activities that Cheapskates may share:

- Hanging the washing outside to dry on fine days rather than using the dryer
- Saving coins in a jar
- Turning lights off when you leave a room
- Grabbing meat markdowns if you are shopping for dinner that night
- Cooking more than one thing at a time in the oven to save on power costs
- Putting leftovers from dinner into a container for tomorrow's lunch
- Looking in the discount shops for some items
- Sorting and passing on the kids' clothes at the end of each season
- Checking for markdowns in the supermarket
- Adding an extra jumper rather than running the heater on full
- Buying fruit and vegetables in season as it saves money and gives the family fresh vitamins and minerals
- Buying Christmas and birthday presents when the sales are on and putting them aside (this not only saves money but helps avoid the hassle of shopping in the Christmas Crush)
- Turning off the hotplate, or at least turning it down, once the pot has come to the boil and letting the vegies sit to steam
- Putting the vegie peelings into a compost bin for garden mulch to help the environment

- Sewing buttons back on and mending or repairing clothes
- Overlocking the frayed edges of towels, face washers and bathmats as the hems unravel and re-using them or using them as dusting cloths or blankets for the pets
- Putting old sports socks into the cleaning cupboard to use as dusters
- Using white vinegar as a cleaner instead of hundreds of other more expensive cleaning products
- Using a toothpaste roll-out to keep the toothpaste neat and to get that last bit out of an almost-empty tube
- Cooking from scratch rather than ordering home delivery or getting takeaway
- Recycling plastic bags by using them for rubbish or storage in the fridge or freezer
- Putting food into plastic containers rather than using plastic wrap
- Turning almost-empty sauce bottles upside down to get the last drop from the bottle
- Rinsing tomato soup tins to get every last bit or scraping out the cream container with a spatula
- Using butter wrappers to grease cake tins
- Checking the price of petrol and filling up when it's lowest for the week
- Automatically comparing prices and sizes.

If you answered yes to any of these you are already on your way to being a Cheapskate. Congratulations!

Now, take a look through this book. It's full of practical, easy-to-follow tips that you can use every day—and many are fun. There are numerous ideas that will save you time, effort and money each time you use them. Why not add a new Cheapskate way every week for the next year. We guarantee that you will save hundreds of dollars or more, have more money to buy the things you really want and have a great time in the process. Give it a go and enjoy the savings. It takes a little effort, but the rewards are worth it. Truly, this is the best New Year's resolution that you can give yourself—so whether it's January, October or March, come and be a Cheapskate and get back your life.

Remember, we love to hear your stories—we have received emails from thousands of people. Let us know how being a Cheapskate has changed your life by visiting our website:

www.cheapskates.com.au/cheapskatesway

Part 1:

CHEAPSKATE
ways to live

A Better Life

According to the Australian Bureau of Statistics, Australians today are twice as wealthy as they were thirty-seven years ago. This information comes as no surprise: our homes are larger and furnished more luxuriously and our cars are bigger, faster and more comfortable. We also have more cars per household, we travel further and more often for our holidays, eat out regularly and follow fashion more closely. With this increase in wealth, however, has come an increase in debt. We are now a nation with alarmingly high personal and national debt. Likewise, we have forgotten how to save and how to plan a budget and then live by it!

Banks encourage us to live on credit. It has never been easier to borrow money. We are flooded with offers for credit cards with larger limits, personal loans, cash advances and credit. Our TV screens constantly promote spending and we have become dependent on debt to survive. For many people this is a downward spiral and as they struggle with high credit card and personal debt, home loan rates are on the rise and petrol takes more of the weekly budget than ever before.

Live within Your Means

You have to bite the bullet and decide to live within your means. Put simply, that means if you have $500 coming into your household each week, you ensure that you spend only $490. Now, that may alarm you, but we are here to help you learn ways to make living within your means easier. First, we need to get a snapshot of where you are now. You could go and spend more money to have someone tell you what you already know—and a financial planner or a

budgeting expert can do that, but so can you. By taking responsibility, you have the power to change your spending habits.

Take Charge of Your Money

1 Work out your income

Calculate how much money comes into your household. You can choose to do this on a weekly or fortnightly basis. Remember to:

- Look at how much you get in the hand
- Include any regular income from family payments, interest, dividends or rental revenue, etc.

This will establish your net income.

See the handy Cheapskates Budget Planner on page 236.

2 Work out your expenses

Calculate how much money goes out. Try to work this out so that it corresponds with the interval you chose for your income. Remember to:

- List all your regular expenses, such as rent, loan repayments, credit card repayments, school fees, etc.
- Add your utility costs, such as electricity, gas, water, telephone, mobile phones
- Include transportation costs to work, such as train fares, petrol, car services, parking, etc.
- Include insurances, car registration, health insurance, etc.
- Add your food bills and entertainment costs
- Use your bank and credit card statements for the last few months to find any other regular expenses you have and how much they are.

Make a long list of all the expenses and include their total. While this may be a daunting exercise, it allows you to actually see where all your money is going. Yes, it may make you feel a little uncomfortable, but please keep in mind that with this information you are armed to make the changes that will get you out of debt and on the road to saving money.

3 Limit your expenses

Now the fun begins. Zoom down your expenses list and mark:

- Essential expenses with a (1)
- Totally optional expenses with a (2).

Calculate your essential expenses. Remember, these have to be below your total income level. If there are some optional expenses that have crept into this category, such as $120 for haircuts each month, fishing tackle for $150 or restaurant and fast food bills for $320 per month, then move them back to the optional category where they belong.

Take your total income and deduct the essential expenses; the money that is left over is how much you have to spend on your optional expenses.

Now look seriously at all of your optional expenses to see what you can eliminate to ensure that you live within your income. To do this takes some serious thought and we have lots of ideas to decrease your expenses—both essential and non-essential.

4 Record all transactions

You can set up your budget on a spreadsheet on your computer or in a ledger book. Make columns so that you can list each item on a new line and add it to your income or expense column. Ensure that you record every transaction. This way each month you can see where all your money is being spent. For example, if you are buying lunch every day, it is a good wake-up call at the end of the month to realise that you have spent $140.

Don't forget to add small annoying fees, such as bank fees or late payment fees. Again, these help you to make better decisions. Your bank fees might be totalling $40 per month, which is nearly $500 per year. This can be the catalyst to make you change banks and move to an account-fee-free bank.

There are many free budget software programs available on the internet. Check out, for example, ww.freeplanner.com.au or www.choice.com.au

Remember: developing a budget isn't a punishment. It gives you greater freedom by placing you in control of your money—and it ensures you don't get caught in the debt trap. If you are already in debt, budgeting will give you the power to get out of debt and back in control of your life.

5 Check your progress

Every month you need to sit down and take a look at your progress. Some months things may slip and you will overspend in some areas. By checking your progress, you get a chance to jump on any bad habits and bring them back in line.

6 Try a new saving strategy each month

Keep this book handy so that each month you can decide on a new saving strategy for the family to try. Maybe last month you introduced the fabulous Cheapskates' laundry tips, thereby reducing your laundry bill by $7 per month. This month consider changing your shopping habits and introduce two new petrol-buying strategies.

7 Involve the whole family

Don't try to be a martyr. If the family is overspending, then everyone has to work together to save money. The children can help by reducing shower times or not asking for expensive advertised takeaway food. Dad can make and take his lunch to work four days a week and mum can change to a hairdresser who charges $25–$50 for a haircut, not $120.

One of the best ways to enrol the children in your new savings program is to share the planning with them. Most children over ten can learn how to budget. Younger children can learn how to budget their pocket money. Not only will your financial situation improve, you will have taught the children a valuable life lesson. The time you spend together as a family will bring you all closer together as you work towards your common goals. Maybe your dream is to go on an overseas holiday or to renovate so the children don't have to share a bedroom or bathroom. Whatever your goals are, save as a family and living the Cheapskate way will become a habit.

Your family budget

Making ends meet is a challenge for many Australian families. One of the most important tools to help you meet that challenge is a good spending and saving plan, with a budget designed especially for your family by your family. Your budget is a guide for dividing up your income so that it provides for your needs and as many of your wants as possible. A budget can help you:

- Spend within your income
- Place your needs above your wants
- Set aside money for large planned expenses and emergencies
- Save and get the things you want
- Reduce (or avoid) family arguments about money
- Purchase the same amount as you are now or more for less money
- Be debt-free
- Save to secure your future
- Make your dreams come true.

Being a Cheapskate reduces your stress and increases your fun. It restores your peace of mind and over time gives you the lifestyle you can afford to keep living.

For more information

For the latest downloadable tip sheets, budget templates and website resources and great online calculators go to our website:

www.cheapskates.com.au/cheapskatesway

Managing Your Money

Is there too much of the month left when you come to the end of your pay? Do you withdraw $100 or $200 from the ATM only to find that you don't have anything to show for it three days later? Money management is not a specific skill, rather it is about your attitude towards money.

 Be a Great Money Manager—Change your attitude. I haven't always been great at budgeting and saving. A family crisis changed my attitude and put me on the path to a debt-free life and a secure financial future.

If your goal is financial freedom and control of your money, there are five characteristics you need to develop:

1. Paying your bills when they are due
2. Ensuring your assets exceed your liabilities
3. Not incurring any new debt
4. Sticking to your payment plan to reduce debt
5. Being content with what you have right now.

Making ends meet

These days we see people on TV sharing their stories of the terrible levels of debt they are carrying. You hear them say time and time again that they can't make ends meet. At the *Cheapskates Journal* we constantly receive emails, letters and phone calls begging for help. So, we have put together the Cheapskate tips to help you begin saving money immediately.

Spend less than you earn

The first decision that has to be made is to spend less than you earn. Making some simple adjustments to the way you spend can get you on the path to investing and saving—with very little effort on your part.

Super Savings Hint: *I love a good cappuccino or cafe latté; however, the price of them makes me grimace. To enjoy my daily coffee fix costs $3.45 and that totals a massive $24.15 per week or a frightening $1259.25 per year. Ouch! Guess what I got for Christmas from my thoughtful mum? Yes, a wonderful coffee machine. We buy our coffee from our local coffee shop and make our own cappuccinos. The coffee costs $15 for a large bag that lasts three weeks. This saves me $57.45 every three weeks or an incredible $999.25 per year! Now I get to drink the coffee I love and save $1000 a year.*

The point is simple: being a Cheapskate is all about having the luxuries you enjoy in a way that is affordable.

Simple ways to make a difference
Yoghurt packs

Do your kids love yoghurt in their lunch boxes? You can save approximately $2.50 a week by buying a 1-kilogram container of yoghurt and spooning it into small resealable snack cups. This equates to a saving of $130 a year if you have just one tub of yoghurt a week. For a family with two or three children, you can save even more.

uper Savings Hint: *Watch your supermarket catalogues and shelves for sale prices on yoghurt. As long as it has a good shelf life (yoghurt usually has a shelf life of one month), buy up for the next month while on sale. You can save between 80 cents and $1 when it is on sale, so buying for the next month can save you $4. Our local supermarket has one of the yoghurt brands on sale every six weeks, so, I can save $4 every six weeks—or $32 each year. While the children have their favourites, we mix and match for variety and enjoy the savings.*

Buying your lunch

If you normally spend $7 a day on your lunch, taking a packed lunch from home can save you a lot of money. Packing a sandwich, snack, fruit and drink is not only cheaper, but healthier, too—so the savings will come back to you in the form of fewer medical expenses. You can easily save over $1000 each year just by taking your lunch. Buying your lunch for around $7 per day for five days a week for forty-six* weeks a year costs $1610 per year. (*This is calculated on fifty-two weeks a year, less four weeks' holiday, less public holidays and sick days, which equals 46 weeks.)

If there are two working in your family, buying lunch can double this figure. Likewise, giving the children money for lunch each day or a snack after school can add up to a huge amount of money. Imagine how much you are spending with mum and dad buying lunch and giving the children tuckshop money—it is likely to be over $5000. Wow, imagine the holiday you could have with

$5000! The average family can save $1000–$4000 living the Cheapskate way.

Over $2000 savings

So, with just a few simple changes to the way you spend, you could quite easily save a grand total of $2129.25 in one year! This can go towards a family treat, a new car or paying off your home loan.

Quick Cheapskate Ways To Save Money—Grate a bar of soap and dissolve it in water instead of buying soap powder. You'll only need to use a very little to get the washing clean. This can be used in top-loading and front-loading machines (you only need a teaspoon for front-loading machines).

Cook and bake instead of buying. Empty the freezer and use up all those mystery packages. Make every night a surprise dinner night.

Use a cup cake tin to make muffins—you'll get more from the recipe.

Before hitting the supermarket, shop at home. Is there anything in the pantry that you can use up? Be creative; you may come up with a future family favourite.

Mix powdered garlic, dishwashing detergent and water to use as an insecticide spray for plants.

Essential and non-essential spending

The most common reason people end up in out-of-control debt is that they confuse essential and non-essential spending.

Essential spending includes:
- Rent/mortgage
- Utilities: gas, electricity, phone, water (but you can save here too)
- Food (but shop at home first)
- Medical/pharmacy (don't skimp on serious medical conditions)
- Petrol: unless you can walk everywhere, you'll need your car, but try to limit how far you go and how often you use it. Carpool if you can, share the school run with another mother, do all your errands in one round trip.

Non-essential spending includes:
Everything else. This is where you need to look at saving money. You need to stop buying these items or find cheaper options.

Ways To Save Money

Set up and use a price book

A price book gives you a head start over the chaotic, ever-changing supermarket price game. The concept of a price book may be new to you—it will help you to save money, time and energy and get organised at the supermarket! It's not something that we are taught to use so most of us are unaware of the value it can provide in saving us hundreds of dollars each year. Simply by recording the price of every item you buy, you have a ready reckoner of just where you'll be able to get the very best price. Recording the price for food, whitegoods you are researching or shoes you are thinking about buying can help you to make the right decision about where to spend your money.

Use a small notebook to record your prices. Itemised supermarket dockets are a price book's best friend. On them, you'll find identified and itemised lists of products you buy and use. They will be listed by name and usually have the size or weight included as well as the item price. Jumpstart your price book by recording data from every receipt you can find. For convenience (and your sanity), develop a list of store codes. Use a short abbreviation for each supermarket, discount store and warehouse you shop at regularly. For example in my book Safeway and Woolworths are both W, Coles is C, Aldi is A, Go-Lo is GL, Clint's is Cts, Bi-Lo is B, IGA is IGA, Reject Shop is RJ, and so on.

Now, give each page in your price book an item name; for example, soap powder, corn flakes, milk powder, rice, toilet paper, etc. On this page you will faithfully record the date, store and price for that item, every time you buy it or see it on sale somewhere or in a catalogue.

See page 238 for a sample page.

Keep a calculator handy for unit price calculations! To find any item's unit price, divide the cost of the item by the number of units. Spreadsheet users can short cut the calculation process by breaking out the price and size on the spreadsheet.

So, now that you've scrounged through your purse, handbag and the fruit bowl for dockets and entered your data, it's time to shop.

Like good wine, a price book's value increases with age. At first, you'll be filling in initial entries for many, many product pages but as time passes, the price book's growth will give you a clear view of each item's sale cycle. Build your price book each time you shop. See a great special at Supermarket A, but you don't need the product that week? Record it in your price book anyway. Note the last time it was that price at that store and you'll find their sales cycle. You'll know to return next sale cycle, ready to buy.

With a mature price book, item entries slow. Once you've sampled prices at several supermarkets or discount stores, only enter a new price if it is lower than your existing entries.

As your price book matures, be prepared for surprises! Often, even the dedicated bulk buyer will discover that she's been paying top dollar for bulk goods. No single traditional supermarket has the lowest prices in every area, no matter what their advertising slogans say.

Approach the price book exercise with an open mind; you'll find surprising bargains and high price shocks in the most amazing places. As you shop each week, fortnight or month, note prices in your price book. If any supermarket workers confront you, explain that you are keeping track of prices for your own use when shopping. Be polite, and firm. If they persist, report the staff member and the supermarket to head office. You are shopping in their store, adding to their profits and for that they really should know that the customer is always right.

Ready, set, save!

Over time, you'll build an impressive database of local supermarket pricing information. All around Australia every supermarket has a buy/sale cycle, although it might vary from area to area. You'll soon know that large tins of name-brand coffee will be offered on sale at six-weekly intervals, rotating around the three major supermarkets. You'll know when to stock up on steak, soft drink or diet foods. You'll understand that toilet paper will be offered at twelve for $2.95, for example, every six weeks and you'll purchase six weeks' worth during that buying opportunity.

You'll also know, at a glance, when to buy in bulk and when to look for a better deal. Not all bulk purchases represent true bargains. With your price book, you'll know to the cent when to load up on the big bag of flour and when to pass it up in favour of the supermarket's loss leader—those fantastic bargains (often placed at the front ends of the aisles) that are used to get you in through the door—of the week.

Most of all, a price book will reveal your target price: a realistic, rock-bottom price goal for each item listed in your book. Whether it's cereal for $1.99 per box or detergent at 9 cents per use, you'll have the information you need to know when a bargain is truly a bargain.

Look at your essential items

Food

Buy food at a cheaper supermarket or switch to generic brands, buy and eat more fruit and vegetables than processed food, cook from scratch rather than buying prepared meals. On average fresh fruit and vegetables in season cost one-third less than processed food. Any time you buy something in a packet, container or box that has been processed you are paying much more for it and getting food that has had much of its original nutrients and flavour removed and substituted by food colourings, artificial flavourings and preservatives—none of which are good for you or your children. Try to stick to natural options; they taste better, are much better for you and you save money—often lots of it!

Credit cards or bank loans

Shop around and find a lower interest rate; credit card rates vary enormously and some personal loans offer interest rates as high as 35 per cent. There is plenty of information on the internet or go to your local library and read *Money Magazine* to find information about the banks that offer the best deals.

Shop for better telco rates

Stop using your mobile phone or move to a prepaid card and set a strict budget. Take a look at your internet bill; can you get a better deal now? Switch to a telco that will give you a deal for your landline, mobile and internet. You can easily save $100 a month on all these bills by shopping around.

Look at your non-essential items

Here is a quick list of things you could eliminate or substitute with a cheaper option:

Takeaway food

It is cheaper and healthier to prepare your own meals. By the time you drive to the shop, stand in the queue and wait for the food, you could have whipped up something tastier and healthier at home. It is a fallacy that fast food is fast. In actual fact it is often slower and far less tasty than your own cooking.

Haircuts

Spend $25 rather than $125 on your haircuts. Many hairdressers charging $25 will give you a haircut that is as good as the $125 version. Some hairdressers charge more because they can, not because they provide a better haircut. Children's haircuts at $80 are ridiculous, especially when they are just trimming long straight hair. Look for cheaper hairdressers, find a good one and keep going back. You can save $660 per family member simply by changing hairdressers.

Smoking

Not only is smoking unhealthy, it is shockingly expensive. That $4000 can be put into your mortgage to reduce one year from the loan, saving you $4000 in interest fees. Or you can use it to pay off credit cards or invest on the stock market to make $5000. Smoking costs you and your family. It is not worth the $4000 per year you are burning up.

Alcohol

Alcohol is expensive. Whether you are having a few stubbies or mixed drinks or bottles of wine at home or going out to clubs where you pay $5–$8 per glass, it is an expensive way to relax. Instead, take the children and go for a walk in the park, throw a ball or ride the swings. It will save you between $2000 and $3000 every year.

Your car

In the past, it was common practice for people to change their own oil and spark plugs. It can be a good way to relax, to get out and do something that is totally different to your normal work. This may be a great way for you to save $160 every 5000–10,000 kilometres, which, for most cars, will save you between $500 and $1000 every year.

Children's clothes

Look for cheaper children's clothes. While they are infants and toddlers, they go through two or maybe three sizes every year. Spending $30 for a top or $20 for a pair of pants that will only be worn for a few months is unnecessary. You can find great children's clothes that have been hardly worn at all at markets and opportunity shops or buy them second-hand from a friend.

My uncle used to work for a company that made $2 shampoos and $8 shampoos and he said the only differences were in the packaging and scent used. You can save a fortune—try some cheaper brands. Remember: much of the manufacturer's costs come from the expensive TV, radio and magazine advertisements—not the products they put in the bottle!

Gambling

Every time you gamble you give money away—to the company running the gambling venue or to the state government in taxes. You can invest a small amount of money in a bank account every week and by the time your child is twenty they will have thousands of dollars to start them off in life.

Magazines

Magazines are a hidden expense. Sure, they may cost only $5–$10, but many people buy three or four each month. In most cases 50 per cent of the content is advertisements to make you spend more money. Read them at the library for free or read the gossip on free websites on the internet.

When money is tight

When money is really tight there is only one thing to do—buy the essentials that you need and stop or at least dramatically cut back on buying the extras or non-essential items.

Control credit card spending

Australians owe $21 billion in credit card debt. And that is only on the cards issued by Australian banks; it doesn't include American Express, Diners Club, store cards, etc. Now is the time to face facts: we need to reduce the amount of money we owe. If you have long-term credit card debt then it's time to accept that you have to stop spending as much.

Psychologists have given credit card spending the name 'debt denial'. Debt denial is when spenders refuse to admit that they have financial problems. They start to deny the consequences of their actions (or inaction) to the point of no return. Often these people can lose everything they possess, including their family, and end up in serious financial trouble, even bankruptcy. There are places to get help and support if you need it (see page 240); however, the reality is that at some point you will have to take responsibility for your spending. You will have to stop spending and begin to pay the debt off.

Reduce your credit card debt

There are three ways to get out of debt:

Stop spending

It's commonsense really, isn't it? You have to stop buying non-essential items and begin to pay off your credit card—and not just the minimum monthly payment; you have to pay the entire debt back. If you have more than one credit card, look at the interest rates and pay the one with the highest interest rate off first. If the minimum monthly payment is $120, then begin paying $160 per month. Find some Cheapskate ways to save the extra $40 that you are now going to pay off each month. Once you have paid off this card, cut it up and start paying off the next one. Take a look at how much interest you are now saving per month—you can be proud of yourself.

Consolidate credit card debts

Consolidate credit card debts so that you have one loan with a lower interest rate. You can do this, for example, by:

- Putting all the credit card debt onto one card (cancel the rest)
- Approaching your bank and transferring your debt to a personal loan or finding a bank or credit union that may reduce your interest rate from, say, 17 per cent (the rate offered by the main banks' credit cards) to a personal loan for, say, 11 per cent interest. This will save you hundreds of dollars in interest payments and allow you to pay off the loan sooner. Arrange for the payment to be automatically deducted from your bank account each payday so you don't miss any payments and incur extra charges.

- Do note that interest rates fluctuate. Really do your homework on interest rates available at various suppliers—banks, credit card unions, and so on—before making financial decisions.

Consolidate all your debts into your mortgage

If you have enough equity in your home—that is, you owe less than 80 per cent of the total value—you may be able to roll all your debts into your home loan.

> **Super Savings Hint:** *If you consolidate all your debts into your mortgage, you are now paying your debts off over a longer period. You will need to be dedicated and focused on getting the mortgage paid off as quickly as possible otherwise you will end up paying huge amounts of interest. Having your home loan for one extra year can cost you over $2000 in interest.*

Simple saving tricks

If you have a spending problem or you just haven't developed the habit of saving, here are two simple tricks you can use to increase your savings.

Hide it before you can spend it

Out of sight is out of mind—and when it comes to money, out of sight means in the bank. In sight eventually means out of the wallet. So, get your money out of sight before you can spend it. Set up a direct debit transfer from your main bank account to another bank account—one that you don't have a card or chequebook for so that it is difficult for you to get to that money. You will be amazed at how much you can save in a year when you don't notice it. Consider setting up a salary sacrifice system into your superannuation fund, if you're eligible. It is a great way to quickly build your retirement nest egg.

Limit your spending power

Automated teller machines (ATMs) make getting cash very easy. Just take a look at your bank statements. See all those $40, $60 and $100 ATM withdrawals listed? Can you account for that cash? Probably not!

Money Management Tips

Make some withdrawal rules

- Decide on a minimum amount of cash you need for a week
- Withdraw that amount on Monday, and do not make another cash withdrawal until the following Monday
- If something important comes up, use your credit card if you absolutely have to—just remember that you have to pay the bill at the end of the month
- Keep saving for your goals. Every little bit adds up. When you get a windfall—for example, your tax refund or bonus at work—add it to your savings (after you're debt-free, of course!).

Cash not plastic

Leave the plastic at home. Research has shown that when you shop with a little, lightweight, convenient plastic card you spend about 30 per cent more than if you carry and pay by cash.

Piggy bank

A quick, painless and easy way to start saving is to, at the end of each day, put all your loose change into a piggy bank or a coffee jar or something similar. It quickly adds up over the week or month and you'll be surprised just how much you can save using this method.

 My brother has done this every night for years and it is the way he saves for his annual holiday. Imagine $10 a week for fifteen years: that's $7800 saved, plus any interest earned! And you won't even have missed it.

Save 50-cent coins

Have some family fun: declare that you will all save your 50-cent coins for a family event. Get a special Fifty-cent Box. At the end of the year count the money and use it for your family or holiday treat. Over the course of a year you can save a few hundred dollars.

 One year after we began saving our 50-cent coins, we had saved enough to pay for our two-week holiday—$638 to be exact!

Once a month empty the box, count the money and take it to the bank. The kids love to see the balance grow and they are having fun while learning to save.

Stick to your budget

Withdraw your money for the week and then divide it up according to what has to be paid; that is, petrol, lunches, groceries, music lessons, sports fees, etc. and place it into labelled envelopes.

Carry what you need

Don't put it into your purse or wallet until you are going to pay for that item. This way you will spend only the money allocated to that activity and you can be confident that you have it when it's needed.

Smart saving

Open an account at a bank or financial institution you don't use. Set up an automatic deduction straight from your pay to credit your new savings account. Don't get ATM or internet access to the account so you have to go to the bank to make a withdrawal. Limited access is a great way to save.

$100/24-hour rule

The $100/24-hour rule is great to help you ward off temptation. Put simply, if you're tempted to buy something that is more than $100, commit to waiting for 24 hours before buying it. During that time carefully weigh up your options:

- Do you really need it?
- Do you have the cash on hand?
- Will you need to borrow from the budget?
- Will you have to go into debt to buy it (credit cards, store loans etc)?

- Can you raise the money to buy it (work some overtime, garage sale, use birthday money, etc.)? Most of the time you'll change your mind when you realise how much it will really cost you to buy it on credit. This simple little exercise can save you a couple of years' worth of debt repayments!

Lunches, snacks and drinks

Cancel the coffee on the way to work, take your lunch from home, and make dinner each evening. Stop spending money on extra food when you already have a fridge, freezer and pantry full of things to eat at home. Reduce bought lunches by at least one and save $7 per week and don't buy snacks and drinks on shopping trips for you or the kids and save at least $10 per week. Don't go out for coffee and save another $3 per week . . . altogether that saves at least $1040 per year!

Bargain buys

Allow a set amount of money each week for bargain buys. Stock up on extra-cheap margarine (and freeze it), soap powder, toilet paper, etc. This way you will always be able to take advantage of a great buy without putting a strain on your budget. Put the extra money you begin to have in subsequent weeks into paying off your credit card debt or mortgage.

Aqua fill

Water is the best thirst quencher there is—it's better for you, is already on hand and is much, much cheaper than soft drinks or cordials. Did you know that studies have shown that tap water in most Australian cities is better for you than bottled water? It has fluoride for reduced tooth decay and has fewer impurities. Don't waste money on bottled water—some of it is straight out of the tap anyway.

Money-saving meals

Omelettes, spaghetti Bolognese, macaroni cheese, stir-fried vegies, toasted sandwiches, soup or fried rice are all meals that can be made quickly and cheaply with food that you already have in the house.

Out of bread? Make scones for lunch or add them to the top of a stew —they are quick, easy and filling and stretch out a meal. In our house we make Surprise Stew—all the leftovers in the fridge are put into the slow cooker with a tin of tomatoes, a tin of tomato soup and a topping of scones. Cooked on low all day, it's delicious for dinner, and virtually free, since it's made from leftovers.

Learn the secrets to stretching meals: more vegies, less meat. Cut the meat portions in half and fill up on vegies. Use bread, scones or dumplings to stretch the meal further. Add TVP* (Textured Vegetable Protein) to a casserole, stew or pasta sauce and you can double the quantity without doubling the cost.

Transport

Petrol prices are skyrocketing and have been as high as $1.50 per litre. Consider other means of transportation: walk the kids to school, walk to work, ride a bike or catch the bus or train to work. Think of ways you can leave the car in the garage for those short, regular trips.

---

*TVP is available in most supermarkets or health food shops.

Cent challenge

Play a game: see how long you can go without spending a cent. Rise to the challenge and payday won't seem so far away.

Present buying

When you're not organised and rushing at the last minute to buy Christmas or birthday presents, you end up paying a lot more for the gifts. Instead, shop throughout the year at department store sales, garage sales, op shops and markets, and don't forget mail order catalogues and fairs and fetes.

Conserve water

Fix that dripping tap, install a low-flow showerhead and reduce showers to three minutes. You'll not only be saving a precious resource, but about $125 if not more per year.

How to Get More Out of Your Day

A day is only twenty-four hours long. You can't put more hours in your day but you can certainly get more out of every hour. The Cheapskate way of being organised and efficient in everything you do will help to give you more time to do the things you want to do.

Do it now

Don't let chores stack up: deal with them straightaway and once completed, move on to the next task. It takes less time and energy to complete a task than to start, restart and complete the task later. For example, fold and put away the clothes as you take in the washing, file documents or pay bills as you do the mail, wash the dishes after the meal, put the groceries away after shopping.

Use a diary

Buy a new diary—it can be an 85-cent student diary, a $20 one or an electronic version—school diaries are useful as they have school holidays included. List important dates, activities, sports events and other information, such as phone numbers, carry it with you everywhere and add appointments as needed.

Family calendar

Keep the family organised by using a large wall month-to-month calendar, which you can download free from the internet. Give each family member a column and a different colour and list all dates and appointments on the calendar so that they can be seen clearly.

Daily routine

Set up a family routine and stick to it. Life's much easier when it is planned. Have routines for mornings, after school, evenings and weekends. The routine needs to include all the chores, such as housework and homework, dinner plans and bedtimes.

To-do list

Have a to-do list. Before you go to sleep at night take a minute to jot down the things you need to do the next day. Use a small spiral notebook so you can carry it with you. Cross off all the things you get done each day with pride. If it isn't on your to-do list, then it won't get done.

Address book

Have a complete and up-to-date address book. Write details in pencil so that they can be changed. Don't forget to include email addresses, postal addresses and mobile phone numbers. This will save you lots of time looking up numbers and addresses.

Filing system

A simple filing system can save your sanity and money. Use a filing cabinet or label a box and use manila folders. Label the folders: Warranties, School Papers, Electricity Bills, Phone Bills, Insurance, Rates, Car, etc. Then when you get a piece of paper relating to a folder—pay it and file it!

Don't overbook your day

Use the 80 per cent rule to avoid cramming too much into your day! Book up 80 per cent of your day leaving time in between tasks and appointments. This will leave you a few moments if urgent tasks pop up. With things running smoothly you will get a few minutes' breathing time.

Make a waiting bag

Have things to do when you are caught waiting for someone or something. You may be left on hold, sitting in the dentist's office or at the station waiting for your train. Keep a small file or bag with some things you can do. If you use all of your time, you'll fit more in. You can include all manner of things in your waiting bag: a book to read; a scarf you are knitting for your son; stationery and stamps for a letter; Christmas cards or birthday cards to write out or your cheque-book to pay your bills. Always have your waiting bag ready to go with you.

Plan and organise

Plan and organise your time. If it is not working one way, try another. You might try notepads, diaries, whiteboards, cork boards, electronic organisers or computer programs. Don't forget to use colour—stickers, fun pens or Textas.

Organise Your Time

15-minute blocks

A useful tip for any new Cheapskate is to block your tasks into 15-minute intervals. This makes it easy for you to schedule what you have to do in your day and will keep a subtle amount of pressure on you to get things done quickly and efficiently.

Group things

Group things together into 15-minute blocks (see page 239 for a sample Time Block Chart). For example, when you are in the kitchen cooking, use that time to empty the dishwasher or set the table, too, or while you are on the computer checking emails, make phone calls or diary entries while waiting for downloads. (And remember to answer your emails straightaway!) Having a set time in which to complete tasks makes it easier to finish them according to plan and on time.

Specific times

Set aside specific times for completing certain tasks and don't let phone calls interrupt you (unless it's an emergency or one of the children), instead allow the calls to go to the answering machine. Block in 15 minutes to return the calls.

Say no

Learn to say no. It is easy. You don't need to offer an explanation; in fact, if you do, you are leaving yourself open to be offered an alternative. Just say no, and then change the subject. If you have organised and planned your day—stick to your plan.

Easy to find

Are you forgetful or do you tend to lose things? Write your name, address and phone number on all your easy-to-lose possessions.

Make your own labels or buy iron-on stickers to ensure your and your children's possessions are easy to identify, find and return.

Functional rooms

Make it a point to use each room for the function for which it was designed. This means don't take your shoes off in the lounge room and don't eat in the bedroom. You will have less mess and keep the house tidy.

Work in time

Work with a time limit: do a job by time. Set the timer on your stove or better still put on a CD. Plan to work for only two or three songs, just long enough to get the job done. If you have a big job, put on the '1812 Overture', that should give you enough time and enthusiasm for a huge job.

Double-up entertaining

If you are going to entertain, invite guests on back-to-back days or have twice as many people. This makes one evening, one lot of cooking and one big clean-up.

Wasted time

Reduce the time you waste looking for things. Have a hook for keys just inside the front door, add a shelf and a file for bills. Teach children to put their shoes in their wardrobe or on a shelf by the door. Remember: time equals money!

Downsize

Sometimes it's difficult to get rid of our stuff, even if we never use it. Rather than throwing it out, give it to a friend or someone in need. Donate the things you don't use to a homeless shelter, charity, op shop or church. Rather than having it take up space, give it to someone who really needs it.

Prioritise

Italian economist Vilfredo Pareto documented the 80-20 Rule. It says that 80 per cent of the reward comes from 20 per cent of the effort. Identify your important tasks and prioritise your time to concentrate on those tasks first. Use coloured tags, numbers or letters to flag your priorities.

Shopping

Buy in Bulk

Buy frequently used household items, such as toilet paper, soap, tissues, shampoo, conditioner and paper towels, in bulk and save money, time and energy. This is another great strategy to reduce the number of trips you make to the supermarket.

Be Sensible and Save

Know your prices

Do your research. Check your prices to ensure that they are cheaper. Just because you buy in bulk does not ensure that you will make savings: some foods are cheaper when the supermarket has a sale.

Super Savings Hint: *Nescafé Coffee is often on sale for $12.95 for a 500-gram tin. Buying two tins on sale is cheaper than buying a 1-kilogram tin costing $39.95. The larger tin is $14 dearer. Wait for the sale and buy enough to last for two to three months as that is the current on-sale cycle for this product in the supermarket.*

Do you need/use it?

Only buy items that you actually need and use. It is a false economy to buy something you don't need no matter how good the price is; the money is better saved for something special!

Buying perishables

Buying anything perishable in bulk isn't always a good idea. It can often go off before you have a chance to finish using it and this wastage costs you money. If you buy perishables in bulk consider freezing, bottling, dehydrating them or sharing them with a friend.

Bulk Buys

Toilet paper for 20 cents a roll
15kg case of apples for $19.95 rather than 1kg for $3.95
Plastic wrap
Laundry detergent
A4 printer paper
Coffee on special
Jars of baby food on special
Soft drink on special
Car oil
Shampoo and other hygiene products
Herbs and spices
Chocolate and treats

Cooking supplies

The next best items to stock up on are daily cooking supplies, such as salt, olive oil, spices, flour, sauces and sugar, which store well and keep for a very long time. If you cook on a regular basis it saves money to buy these ingredients in bulk.

Beans

Dried beans can last for several years if you keep them moisture-free in an airtight container. Beans are great value for money as they are an excellent source of protein and are a good filler in soups, stews and casseroles. Remember, you can use them whole or whiz them into a pulp to add to your meal.

Drinks
Most juices that you buy, such as apple juice, can last three to five years unopened. If you are unsure of how long your juice will last, contact the manufacturer.

Warehouse outlets/direct sales
Warehouse outlets and direct sales from manufacturers or importers often offer great value for money, especially when you buy in bulk. Remember to always carry your price book so you know what you should be paying—don't get caught up in the deal and pay too much.

Compare apples with apples
As the saying goes, make sure you are comparing apples with apples. This may mean that you need to compare the can size by figuring out how much each gram costs. For example, a large can of tomato paste may work out to be 5 cents per gram yet the smaller can is 9 cents per gram. Obviously the larger one is cheaper if you use a lot of tomato paste. Alternatively, it may be how many items are in the packet or how many litres in the container. Don't be afraid to carry a small calculator with you.

Frequently used items
Choose and buy products that your family uses in large amounts. Consider things like peanut butter and canned tomatoes, which are

frequently used. It is great to buy these in bulk as you can save money and have a ready supply. Bulk buying can give you peace of mind as you'll always have something on hand to make. Grab some minced beef from the freezer and you can whip up something that can feed a family who have called in without warning and are staying for dinner or the football team your son has invited home for you to feed.

What To Buy in Bulk

Tinned foods: soups, fruit, vegetables, tuna, salmon, baked beans, spaghetti, pasta sauces, tomato paste, etc.

Paper products: tissues, toilet paper, paper towel, paper plates, feminine hygiene, wrapping paper, cards, copy paper, etc.

Cleaning supplies: soap powder, bleach, laundry soaker, soap, cleaning cloths, fabric softener, fabric spray, etc.

Toiletries: toothpaste, shampoo, conditioner, hair gel, hair spray, toothbrushes, toilet soap, shower gel, etc.

Dry goods: flour, sugar, salt, pasta and noodles, rice, pastry mix, rolled oats, breakfast cereals, herbs and spices, etc.

Freezer foods: mince, steak, roasts, sausages, chicken, chicken fillets, chicken pieces, fish, pies, pasties, sausage rolls, vegetables, etc.

Fresh produce for preserving: apples, oranges, stone fruits, potatoes, carrots, tomatoes, pumpkins, onions, etc.

How long does food last?

Review the average life or shelf life of the products you bulk-buy to ensure that they are consumed before their expiry date.

Frozen Meat and Poultry—Uncooked

Chicken/turkey: 9 months

Steak, beef: 6–12 months

Chops, pork: 4–6 months

Chops, lamb: 6–9 months

Roast, beef: 6–12 months

Roast, lamb: 6–9 months

Roast, pork or veal: 4–6 months

Stewing meats: 3–4 months

Minced meats: 3–4 months

Organ meats: 3–4 months

Frozen Dairy Products

Butter/margarine: 6–9 months

Cheese, soft and spreads, dips: 1 month

Cheese, hard or semi-hard: 6 months

Ice-cream: 1 month

Milk/cream: 3 weeks

Eggs: do not freeze in their shells. Instead break the eggs and stir to
    break the yolk, then pour into icecube trays and cover when
    frozen. Or freeze in serving sizes. Freeze for up to 9 months.

Frozen Fruit and Vegetables

Commercially frozen fruits: up to 1 year

Commercially frozen vegetables: up to 8 months

Dried Items

Baking powder/bicarb soda: 18 months

Breadcrumbs: 6 months

Cereals: 6 months

Flour/cake mixes: 1 year

Gelatine/pudding mixes: 1 year

Herbs/spices: 6–12 months

Milk, non-fat dry: 6 months

Pancake/pastry mixes: 6 months

Pasta/noodles: 2 years

Potatoes, instant: 18 months

Rice, white: 2 years

Sugar, granulated: 2 years

Sugar, brown: 4 months

Optional Items

Chocolate, unsweetened: 18 months

Coffee, vacuum-packed: 1 year

Milk, UHT: 1 year

Nuts: 8 months

Oils/salad dressings: 3 months

Peanut butter (unopened): 6 months

Sauces, condiments, relishes (unopened): 1 year

Shortening: 8 months

Syrups: 1 year

Tea: 18 months (sealed to retain freshness)

Storage Issues

Do you think buying in bulk is a great idea but wonder where you can store the goods? The good news is that even the tiniest house has lots of potential storage space.

Under beds

Do you have space under the beds or has it been taken over by dust bunnies and odd socks? Clear out under the beds and pack away toilet rolls, tissue boxes, cartons of baked beans and the dozen bottles of shampoo that you just bought.

Tops of cupboards

Look on the top shelf of the linen cupboard and tidy up the photo albums, jigsaw puzzles and those loose light bulbs. See how much space there really is? Now you have room for the tinned fruit and the long-life milk.

End tables

Use the space under end tables to store cartons of tinned food. Drape the table with a cloth and no one will know it's actually your bulk storage area.

The roof or garage

Put a sheet of chipboard across the rafters in the garage and store cartons up there. If you have the space, use your ceiling cavity. You may also consider converting roof space into a small attic for storage.

Share with friends

Ask a friend, sister or your mum if they would like to buy in bulk with you. Agree on how much you both want and split the costs accordingly.

Consider bottling

Another storage option for perishable bulk items is to bottle them. If you plan to buy in bulk on a regular basis, it would be a good investment to consider purchasing a bottling outfit to ensure the food is kept airtight.

Smart Shopping

Play off the major supermarkets

Most people have access to at least two local supermarkets. Both will be vying for your trade through weekly advertised specials. Use your price book to compare the prices and enjoy the savings and shop for the cheaper products in both supermarkets. It may take you an extra twenty minutes but you are likely to save $30–$50 on an average shop.

Remember independent stores often have great sale items. Take a look around at the options available in your area. Shopping at the local fresh fruit supplier and butcher can often provide you with fresher food at a cheaper price.

Local markets

Consider shopping at your local markets for fresh produce. They are great for fruit and vegetables and some may have eggs, cheese, meat, plants and flowers. You will be pleasantly surprised by the variety and the prices. Give some of the exotic fruits a try. You can make up some fun ways to taste them with the children. Remember that buying fresh from the market usually means that your fruit and vegies are fresher and will have a longer shelf life.

Buy your staples in bulk. A 10-kilogram bag of potatoes costs around $8 at the markets while major supermarkets are charging $1.98 for 1 kilogram—that's more than twice the price! It's the same for onions. You can buy a 10-kilogram bag for around $4. That is 40 cents a kilogram. If onions are $2.98 for a 2-kilogram bag at the supermarket—you'll save $1.09 a kilogram!

To save time (and tears), mince half of the onions in a food processor and freeze them in ½-cup portions in zip-lock bags (placing them flat to save space). Slice the other half and freeze in 1-cup portions in zip-lock bags. When you need onions, pull them out and use them. You don't need to thaw them.

Bargain time

You can scoop some real bargains just before closing time at the markets. The vendors do not want to pack up, cart and store any remaining produce, so they will drop the prices. It is fun to see them shouting their cheaper prices trying to compete with the next fellow.

Orchards/farm-gate stalls

Keep your eyes open for fruit and vegetable stalls while out enjoying a Sunday drive. Or if you are lucky enough to live near a farm or orchard, you can buy direct from local growers. You will save a bundle and your family will enjoy fresh fruit and vegetables.

Farmers' markets

These fabulous markets are becoming more and more popular and you'll find the most amazing variety there. They are usually held on a Saturday or Sunday—weekly, fortnightly or monthly. They can be semi-commercial, hobby or home-grown farmers. The produce is fresh, prices are good and most of the stallholders have a vast knowledge of their produce. They enjoy sharing their knowledge about how to cook a vegetable or serve a fruit. It is exciting and interesting to learn from them.

Dollar shops/discount stores

Discount shops have some real bargains. Often the packaging or display may look odd, but the contents are generally the same as the brand-name item in the supermarket. If you're not sure, check the ingredients and where it's made with the label on your regular product. You'll most likely find they are almost the same, if not identical. Some of the things you'll save on are tinned soups, instant noodles, cordials, soft drink, sweets, soap powder, shampoo and conditioner, biscuits, chocolate, make-up, bubble bath, pet food and cleaning products.

Bartering

Ever heard of the barter system? You know, where you trade goods or services for the things you need? Well, why not barter for your grocery supplies? If you have a vegetable garden full of tomatoes and you need eggs, trade with your cousin who has hens, but no vegie patch! Or swap lemons for lawnmowing, rhubarb for parsley, etc. And don't stop with family and neighbours. If you have an overabundance of something in your garden, approach your local greengrocer. Chances are if you can provide them with a saleable quantity of produce, they'll take it from you. You could end up with a few weeks' worth of fruit and vegetables for virtually nothing!

Make a deal

The age-old art of haggling seems to have been lost in our day-to-day shopping. Somehow, somewhere we stopped asking for the best deal and it is costing us all money. Shopkeepers have to make money to stay in business, but the norm is to mark up products by 50–200 per cent, depending on the items. This means that often there is a reasonable profit margin and for those who ask, they can receive discounts and bargain prices for the goods and services they want to buy.

The basics of haggling

The bigger the ticketed price, the more important it is to haggle. Most people understand the importance of negotiating on the price of their new house or car. In fact, we all understand that we have to beat the car dealers down on price, but many of us do little negotiating/bargaining/haggling when it comes to other items.

Let's look at your role. You should always aim to get the best possible value for money. This means selecting a product that suits your needs and then trying to get the best possible price. Now, consider the salesperson's role—they need to sell you the product. It is not their job to work out if it suits your needs or to give you the best price. In fact, with so many salespeople on commission, it is their role to achieve the highest possible price for their products.

Now that we have that all cleared up, let's look at ways that you can get the best price on the bigger ticket items you are buying. Over the years we have saved thousands and thousands of dollars on everything from small electrical items (such as toothbrushes, hair dryers and can-openers) to whitegoods (such as microwaves, fridges and washing machines); furniture to cars.

Don't be shy

Always ask for a better deal. It is rare for a salesperson to offer you the best price on an item. They may take $5 or $10 off the price when really you could have received $40 or $50 off. The point is, you have to ask. While some places can't always reduce the price, many smart salespeople will find something to throw in to sweeten the deal. For example, a store may not be able to discount an iPod, though a smart salesperson might add a cover or at least give the cover to you at 50 per cent off to get the deal.

Bundling

In some cases you can get a discount simply by buying more than one item and asking for a deal. This can be useful if you need to buy several electrical/electronic or whitegood items at once.

---

uper Savings Hint: *We received 20 per cent off the price of our new lounge suite. That was a $500 saving simply because I asked for a cheaper price. The lounge was ticketed at $2499. I had done my homework and knew that was a competitive price for this lounge. However, being a true Cheapskate, I still asked, 'What's your best price?'. Without missing a beat, he came back with a discount of $150 dollars—an even better price. He went on to say if we ordered today, we could have it in six weeks, as there was a backlog in supply. I looked closely at the one on the floor—it was in brand-new condition. I didn't want to wait so I asked what the price would be if I took the suite off the floor.*

He said he would sell it for $2060. Now I had a massive $439 off the original price. For my final trump card, I asked for a cash price and that lovely young salesman came back with $2000. I could hardly pay for it fast enough.

Total saving: $499 and delivery three days later.

How to Get the Best Deal

Know what you want

Research your item and the price at different stores. Use catalogues, flyers and the internet and don't forget to ask other people where they get their best deals.

Know your limit

Set your budget and stick to it. Take into account delivery time and delivery charges.

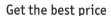

Get the best price

Don't get tricked into telling them what you can afford or how much you want to pay; let the salesperson give you their best price.

Always be polite and friendly

Salespeople don't want to work with aggressive or unfriendly people.

Super Savings Hint: *We received a saving of 22 per cent by combining our purchases. We needed to buy a new washing machine and microwave and had been looking at getting a large freezer. Having done our homework on models and prices we set about getting a great deal by bundling our purchase of all three items together.*

The discounted price for the individual items was $2267. We asked if we could get a better price if we took all three at once. The salesperson quickly did some sums and knocked $435 off the combined price. To see if there was any further discount available, we asked if there was a cash discount. Sure enough, we received a further $80 discount.

Total saving: $515.

Be prepared to haggle

Ask questions; for example:

- How much for cash? (If you are paying cash)
- Do you offer a seniors discount (if it applies)

- Could you please ask your manager if he could do a better price so that I could buy this today?
- Are you sure this is the best price?
- Can you give me free delivery or free installation, etc.

Always be appreciative of a discount. A dollar in your pocket is better than a dollar in someone else's.

Bundle

If you are in the market for other products consider bundling. Ask how much for the total package if you buy two items; for example, a lounge suite and a TV cabinet; washing machine and dryer, etc.

Super Savings Hint: *My mum wanted a new microwave and the kids needed a new electric toothbrush. I found the best price for the microwave oven was $169. I asked what price the salesperson would do if I added an electric toothbrush to the deal. The toothbrush was $59. The salesperson went to ask his manager and returned saying they would do them both right now for a total of $189.*

Total saving: A discount of $30 on the purchase of a microwave and a toothbrush.

Successful Price Negotiating

Find the store manager (or a helpful salesperson who asks the manager).

- Be friendly, not aggressive or grumpy
- Get the salesperson on side (tell a chatty story, for instance)
- Tell them your budget range
- Ask if they guarantee their prices
- Mention that you're a loyal customer
- Offer to pay cash
- Be prepared to buy when your deal goes through
- Be discreet!

January Sales

The January sales are a great time to buy presents for birthdays, Mother's or Father's Day and Christmas. Make a list and keep it with you so that when you see a bargain, you can buy it for the next gift-giving occasion. With a little planning, you can reduce your spending by 30–50 per cent. Most people these days are reported to spend $3000 on average at Christmas alone!

I wait all year long for the January sales. I start making my list of things I need to buy in about February and I add to it throughout the year. I also make a list of gifts I'll need for birthdays and special occasions. I like to put away $10 a week for my January spending spree so then, when I hit the sales, the family budget doesn't really take a beating. The sales usually start on 2 January, but you can get great bargains on 26 and 27 December, too.

It is a good idea to plan your shopping trip. Most stores advertise in papers, catalogues and on TV. Think about what you need and not want you want. It is easy to get caught up in the hype at sale time. Make sure you're wearing comfortable shoes and clothing for the day. Carry a bottle of water in your shopping bag—you don't want to become dehydrated and ill; you might miss a bargain.

January sale time means heavily discounted Christmas goods. Stock up on Christmas cards and gift tags, ornaments and decorations, paper napkins and bon bons. To help you remember where you have stored them come next Christmas just write it on your calendar in November or December.

Remember to go to the food section of the major department stores where you will find plum puddings, Christmas hampers, chocolates and lollies. Check the use-by dates. You may find that some items have a long shelf life, so you can put them in the pantry to use throughout the year.

Summer clothes are also heavily discounted at this time of year. Don't buy anything that you wouldn't have purchased if it wasn't on sale; chances are you are not going to wear it.

Another tip to remember is that about four weeks after sale time the larger department stores advertise another 25 per cent off all marked items. This is when you can really purchase some great buys. Look for clothing that is suitable for preschool and school. Purchasing children's clothes for next season is a good idea. If they are a size 2, buying size 3 or 4 and putting them away for the end of the year saves a substantial amount of money. Discount department stores usually have excellent bargains on children's clothing during the January sales. Now is the time to buy school shoes—before the end-of-January rush and while shoe shops are offering a buy-one-pair-get-another-pair-half-price deal.

Manchester is also usually discounted by about 25–30 per cent. If you are in desperate need for new sheets and towels, now might be the best time to purchase some.

A tip when buying sheets: if you buy plain sheets you can replace a worn bottom sheet with a new sheet and retain your set.

Keep an eye out for crockery bargains, especially at the main department stores. They may have up to 50 per cent off the major brands.

If you like crystal and fine china, go to the factory outlet stores and sign up for their mailing lists. You'll be notified of their sales and get to buy before the general public. You can pick up great gifts at up to 80 per cent off the retail price.

If you're looking for electrical or whitegoods now is the time to buy. It pays to do some research and know the regular price of the item, so you'll recognise a bargain when it comes up.

Cleaning

Cleaning the Cheapskate way can save you a significant amount of money. Furthermore, Cheapskate cleaning tips are environmentally and family friendly. Many of today's commercial chemical-based cleaning products can be detrimental to your family's health, resulting in asthma attacks, headaches and difficulty breathing. Being a Cheapskate means using some of the best old-fashioned cleaning methods—ones that your great-grandmother may have used. They worked back then and they work today and they will save you heaps of money and leave your house looking and smelling fresh and clean and, with the hectic lives we live today, many of these ideas will save you time and energy, too.

Encourage the whole family to get involved in keeping the house clean and tidy. It is great to involve the kids—big and small—and teach them how to put away toys and clean bedrooms and bathrooms. It is part of the education needed for when they grow up.

Getting Started

There are many ways to save money on cleaning costs using simple and efficient cleaning products. For some reason many of us seem to think that good cleaning products need to come in a fancy bottle, have a catchy name and an expensive advertising campaign, but this is not so. In most cases the old-fashioned, green and simple ways to clean are superior. Take a look at some of these ideas and see how much you can save.

Essential cleaning tools

It is not expensive to buy the essential tools to keep your home looking clean and neat. We recommend buying cheaper versions or reusing products.

Soft broom is a must-have. While you can use it to sweep the floors, you can also use it to dust cobwebs from walls or dust hard-to-reach tops of cupboards.

Dustpan and brush are essential for quick tidy-ups, sweeping small areas and picking up dust after you have swept. Buy the cheapest one as there is virtually no difference in what they do—pick up dirt.

Squeeze mop Can be cheap or expensive; buy whichever one you prefer.

Swiffer mop is handy. You can buy a Swiffer mop or you can attach an old face washer to your broom (nappy pins work really well for this)—which will do the same job—and use it to swish around tile and hardwood floors.

Buckets can cost $10 or just 89 cents; it's up to you what you pay. You can use your bucket for washing floors, cleaning walls, soaking clothes, carrying weeds, just about anything really.

Vacuum cleaner is another essential. There is a huge range of vacuum cleaners. You need to get a powerful engine to ensure it will suck up dirt. Uprights can be good and we recommend looking for a vacuum that does not use a bag. There are a few options available and they can dramatically reduce the dust that is returned to the air.

Nylon scouring pad These can be purchased cheaply at discount shops. Use one when still dry to clean the shower screen.

Old stockings Rather than discard your laddered stockings or pantyhose, use them to clean the bath and shower areas. It makes a very gentle scouring pad.

Paper towel Generic brands will do fine. They're great for messy cleaning jobs.

Polishing cloths and dusters can be made using old socks, towels, nappies or T-shirts. You can save $30 or more each year simply by doing this.

Squeegees are perfect for cleaning shower screens and windows. Make sure you have one handy if you have small children as they will inevitably spill drinks, and your squeegee can quickly soak the liquid up. Give it a good rinse after any cleaning job so it is ready to go next time. Be sure to buy a squeegee that has a sponge and a rubber blade.

Spray bottles are great for storing cleaning solutions. Recycle old cleaning bottles.

Toilet brushes are essential—have one for each toilet (if possible).

Old toothbrushes are the perfect size for cleaning in tight corners and around the base of taps and spouts. Just be sure to keep them away from the toothbrushes still in use; you don't want any mix-ups!

Essential cleaning products

You don't need to spend a fortune or have hundreds of different products to maintain your house. A few simple ingredients will do the job of hundreds of commercial cleaning products. We have included a shopping list for the Cheapskate cleaner to have on hand. All cleaning products can be purchased from the supermarket, chemist or hardware store, are cheap to buy and most are multipurpose.

Dishwasher detergent Used to lift heavy stains from pots, pans and dishes and oil stains from clothing.

Bicarbonate of soda (sodium bicarbonate, bicarb or baking soda) is a powerful cleaning agent on its own and is even more powerful when combined with other materials such as white vinegar.

Bleach Buy a cheap generic brand in a 2-litre or larger bottle.

Borax is a naturally occurring mineral. Use as a cleaner, laundry whitener and mild disinfectant. Borax is available in the cleaning products aisle of most supermarkets. Note: Borax is toxic so please keep it stored well away from children and animals.

Cloudy ammonia is a fast drying, non-streaky, multipurpose cleaner that is readily available in the cleaning aisle at your supermarket. Use with caution as the fumes are an irritant. Ensure you wear a mask and that the area is well ventilated. If you have a respiratory problem, avoid using it altogether.

Denture tablets This cleaning agent for dentures is good for removing scale in kettles and toilets. It's available in the personal care aisle, near the toothpaste.

Dishwashing detergent Any cheap brand of detergent is fine to use. Use a pre-wash treatment on stains and for general cleaning.

Eucalyptus oil can be bought at supermarkets, chemists, health food and hardware stores. Use eucalyptus oil to remove sticky residue, as an inhalant, a disinfectant and a cleaner. It is toxic, so keep it away from children and pets. It will also damage plants, so beware if using it in the garden.

Gumption A fantastic cleaning paste available in the cleaning product aisle of most supermarkets.

Lavender oil Available from health food shops or suppliers of essential oils.

Lemon juice Either squeeze fresh juice or buy a bottle of lemon juice. A generic brand is often cheaper.

Pure soap flakes Available in the cleaning product aisle of most supermarkets.

Methylated spirits Great for cleaning glass and ceramic tiles.

Pine cleaner Pine-scented disinfectant.

Peppermint oil Available at health food shops and suppliers of essential oils.

Salt A mild abrasive that can be used for absorbing liquid and oil/grease stains. Use with vinegar to clean copper.

Shampoo The cheaper the better. Use as a general cleaner for floors, baths, greasy cooktops and cuffs and collars.

Soap Buy a generic soap from the cleaning aisle. You can pick up five-bar packs for as little as $1.25.

Sugar soap Use this as a 'degreaser'. It's available in the home care section of the supermarket and in hardware shops.

Vanilla extract Available in the cooking aisle, this can be used as a deodoriser.

Vegetable oil Use generic brands.

Vinegar is made from fermented apples, grapes, sugar cane, malt or wine. It is an acid and a mild disinfectant.

Washing soda Often known by the brand name Lectric Soda. You'll find it in the cleaning aisle of your supermarket, but you'll probably have to search for it. It comes in a crystal or powder form, in a clear plastic bag. It is a good water softener.

Homemade cleaning products

Using the simple, everyday ingredients from the essential cleaning products list you can make just about every type of household cleaner you need. Making your own cleaning products takes only a few minutes and can save you $400–$1000 per year, depending on how many you use.

Washing Powder

This can be used in either top-loading machines (use 1 tablespoon) or front-loaders (1 teaspoon). I use generic laundry soap (the old-fashioned kind).

2 cups grated pure soap
1 cup washing soda
1 cup borax
1 x 500g box bicarb soda

Grate soap in a food processor, add remaining ingredients and whiz until mixture is a fine powder.

You will need only a scant tablespoon—barely level—of laundry powder per load. Really dirty clothes get a rub with a bar of soap or a smear of shampoo before going into the machine.

Pre-wash Spray

Mix:

1 cup cloudy ammonia

1 cup water

1 cup shampoo

1 teaspoon eucalyptus oil

Combine ingredients in a bowl and store in a spray bottle. Shake well before spraying collars and cuffs.

Spray and Wipe-style Cleaner

There is one basic cleaning product I make which I use for everything from benchtops to the bathroom. It has a strong smell but cleans very well.

¼ cup bicarb soda

¾ cup cloudy ammonia

½ cup white vinegar

4 litres warm water

2 drops of food colouring (Add for safety reasons. Use blue as this is the colour of most window cleaners. Label the bottle clearly)

Mix all ingredients and store in a large, sealable plastic container. (An old milk bottle is ideal. Remove the label for safety.) Pour into a spray bottle when needed.

Window Cleaner

½ **teaspoon shampoo**

3 tablespoons white vinegar

2 cups water

**1 drop blue food colouring (Add for safety reasons. Use blue as this is
the colour of most window cleaners. Label the bottle clearly.)**

Blend well and store in a spray bottle.

Vinegar Window Cleaner

When washing windows, using newspaper is best.

½ **cup white vinegar**

4 litres warm water

Mix to combine and transfer to a spray bottle. Squirt on windows,
clean and wipe dry with a squeegee.

Scouring Powder

1 cup bicarb soda

1 cup borax

1 cup salt

Blend and store in a container. This scouring agent is for use on
surfaces where you would normally use a powder cleaner, i.e. most
sinks, baths, hand basins and toilets. Do not use it on surfaces
prone to scratching.

Furniture Polish

1 cup vegetable oil
½ cup lemon juice

Pour oil and lemon juice into a spray bottle or jar and stir to combine. To use, dip dusting cloth in polish, blot the oil by folding the cloth over and then dust furniture. Leaves a beautiful finish!

Stainless Steel Cleaner

You can make a stainless steel sink really shine by using either soda water or white vinegar. After use, wipe sink with a damp cloth splashed with soda water or vinegar and dry with a soft cloth. To deep-clean, damp a cloth with water and add a splash of cloudy ammonia or dishwashing liquid. Wipe surface and dry thoroughly to avoid water spots.

Dishwasher Detergent

This is great if you have run out of dishwasher detergent. If you use it on a regular basis, add white vinegar to the rinse cycle every few loads.

1 tablespoon bicarb soda
1 tablespoon borax

Combine bicarb and borax in a bowl and mix well.

Disinfectant Wipes

Use a plastic container with a lid, large enough to hold half a roll of paper towel.

thick roll of paper towel
$\frac{1}{2}$ cup pine cleaner
$1\frac{1}{2}$ cups water

Cut roll of paper towel in half, put it in a container and remove cardboard insert. Mix cleaner and water in a cup and pour it over paper towels, trying not to make it sudsy. Stand overnight or until all towels are saturated. Use as disinfectant wipes in the kitchen and bathroom.

Grime Buster Paste

Use a small dab on a clean rag to clean the bath, basin, shower, benchtops, etc. Rinse and dry with a soft towel.

$\frac{3}{4}$ cup bicarb soda
$\frac{1}{4}$ cup borax
3 tablespoons dishwashing liquid
1 tablespoon white vinegar
35 drops eucalyptus oil

Mix ingredients to a paste in a bowl and store in a sealed container.

Blanket and Doona Wash Recipe

To wash your blankets, use a good-quality wool mix or make your own using this simple recipe:

½ x 700 g packet pure soap flakes
    (Lux Flakes or similar)
1 cup methylated spirits
2½ tablespoons eucalyptus oil

Mix ingredients together and store in a wide-mouthed screw-top jar. Use 1 tablespoon of mixture per garment. Dissolve in a little hot water before adding to lukewarm water to wash. There is no need to rinse.

Being Green and Family Safe

Cleaning with white vinegar

Ordinary white vinegar has to be one of the most versatile cleaning agents: it can clean, disinfect, deodorise, deter pests, remove mould and kill germs and it's environmentally friendly! For example, it costs as little as $1.69 for 2 litres at our local supermarket! White vinegar can take the place of almost all household cleaners—saving you hundreds of dollars a year! Imagine the ease of having only one cleaning item in your cupboard. How much space would that free up? There'd be no more confusion over which product cleans what item.

Vinegar is a strong cleaning product without harmful nasty fumes or toxic chemicals. It is safe to use around children (especially children susceptible to skin irritations, such as eczema or dermatitis, or breathing difficulties, such as asthma and allergies) and pets. By being a Cheapskate, you can reduce your children's exposure to harmful chemicals. The average household now spends between $300 and $600 a year on simple household cleaning products. There are kitchen cleaners and bathroom cleaners, and then there are different cleaners for the shower, the basin, the floor and tiles ... and the list goes on and on. Switching to white vinegar can reduce the cleaning product bill to $50 for the year—and you will have a clean, green, family-friendly home.

Drains

Rinse with hot water first, and then put in the plug (use a plug with a chain or have tongs handy). Fill the sink with hot water (boiling if you can) and add 1 cup of vinegar and $1/2$ cup of bicarb soda. Once the bicarb soda has stopped fizzing, pull the plug and let it flush out your drains. This removes nasty stale odours and will help to prevent build-ups that cause blockages.

Insects and pests

Wipe over benchtops, sinks, tiles, cupboard doors and shelves with undiluted white vinegar to deter ants, cockroaches and other annoying pests. Spray directly onto cockroaches to kill them.

Pots and pans

Clean the copper bottoms of pots and pans by sprinkling with salt and then gently rubbing with a cloth soaked in white vinegar. Rinse well and dry with a soft cloth.

Weeds

Pour undiluted white vinegar over unwanted weeds. The weeds dry out and die within days so you can sweep them away.

Dishwasher rinse aid

Use white vinegar as a rinse aid in your dishwasher and save a small fortune. Your dishes will sparkle and shine and your dishwasher's interior will be clean, too. A bonus is the sweet smell—no more nasty odours in the dishwasher.

Brick fireplaces

Clean your brick fireplace with white vinegar. Spray it on, and use a stiff brush to scrub. Rinse it off with a cloth that has been wrung out in neat (undiluted) white vinegar.

Electric kettles

Pour 3 cups of white vinegar and 2 cups of water into the kettle, boil and leave overnight. Then empty, fill with clean water, boil and empty again, repeat with clean water and it's ready to use.

The Bathroom

Stop pouring money down the drain! Being a Cheapskate can change the way you clean your bathroom—it no longer needs to be one of the most expensive rooms to clean in the house—without skimping on hygiene.

A trick used by some professional cleaners is to clean bathtubs, basins and showers with shampoo. It works wonders. Dirty rings around the tub are gone instantly. The shampoo removes the body oils that cause the bath ring in the same way that it cleans the oil and dirt from your hair.

> **Super Savings Hint:** *Buy a 1-litre no frills shampoo from a local not-quite-right or two-dollar shop for use in the bathroom. It will cost around $1.99 and last for months. And there's a bonus—you'll have a lovely sweet-smelling bathroom.*

Showers

Use a squeegee or sponge to dry shower tiles and glass after use each day and then spray with a light mist of undiluted white vinegar. This will remove soap residue and prevent mildew from forming and you will only ever have to give tiles and shower screens a quick wipe over to keep them sparkling clean.

Clean shower screens with a dry nylon scourer and white vinegar. Rub over the glass with the scourer to remove soap scum and then wipe over with a cloth dipped in white vinegar. You will have a spotless shower screen for one-eighth of the cost of commercial cleaners. This can save you $5–$8 per month.

A showerhead that is really mired in sediment that cannot be completely removed with vinegar needs a heavy-duty treatment. Dissolve a denture-cleaning tablet in a plastic bag of water. Tie the bag over the showerhead so that it is completely immersed in the liquid and attach with a rubber band or twist-tie. Allow to sit for several hours. Remove bag and turn on shower to clear all traces of sediment.

Toilets

Clean your toilet by splashing a slurp of white vinegar in the bowl and leaving it overnight then give it a good scrub with the toilet brush. Another option is to use bleach. Buy a cheap version, pour some around the sides and in the bowl, give it a quick scrub and then leave for one hour or overnight.

For really bad stains in the toilet bowl, turn off the water, flush toilet to empty bowl and pour in bleach. Give this a scrub and then let it stand overnight with the lid closed to minimise the fumes. Give it another scrub before turning on the water and flushing it again.

Use denture cleaning tablets to get a sparkling clean toilet. Just drop 3–4 tablets in the bowl and leave overnight. Give the bowl a good brush and flush in the morning. Repeat weekly, fortnightly or monthly, as needed. Great for removing bore water stains.

Just before you leave to go away on holiday, drop a couple of denture-cleaning tablets in the toilet bowl. This will stop anything from growing in the toilet and prevent the brown watermark that appears. If someone is coming over to water your indoor plants, leave a couple of Steradent tablets out for them to add to the loo after two weeks.

Baths

Clean the bath right after using it, before body oil has a chance to harden. You can even start the cleaning while you are in the tub—although don't use a slippery cleanser. By the way, a small amount of bubble bath in the water helps to keep the tub clean.

Use a scrunched-up stocking and the cheapest shampoo you can find to dissolve the soap scum and grease in the bath.

To remove mould and mildew from the bathtub or in a hard-to-scrub place, soak a cotton ball in bleach and let it sit on the mould for an hour or two. Scrub with an old toothbrush and rinse with warm water. Repeat if necessary.

Hand basins

To keep your bathroom basin clean, wipe it every time you wash your hands. When you notice a little build-up of dirt simply wipe it down with the soap on your hands. Rinse it while you are rinsing your hands and dry it off with an old towel you have just for this purpose.

Taps

To clean taps, towel rails and other bathroom fittings, wipe with a damp cloth or use a mild shampoo, if necessary, and dry immediately. Swipe the bristles of an old toothbrush over some soap and scrub to remove grimy build-up around the base of taps and in hard-to-reach areas.

Exhaust fans

Bathroom exhaust fans fill up with lint very quickly. Cleaning them regularly will keep them efficient, saving you money. To clean your exhaust fan, take the cover and the filter down. Brush the fluff off the filter and soak the filter and the cover in warm, soapy water. Brush over with an old toothbrush, rinse and dry. Alternatively, run the cover and the filter through the dishwasher (top rack please) when you do the kitchen and laundry fans.

Walls

Bathroom walls need to be cleaned regularly to protect the paint. Wipe them down with a solution of sugar soap and water. If they are stained wipe them with Gumption. Rinse with water and dry with a cloth.

To clean tiles and grout, use a nylon scourer or a scrunched-up pair of pantyhose and white vinegar. Spray on white vinegar and scrub over with the scourer, if necessary. Rinse with water and squeegee dry. To keep tiles sparkling clean and streak-free, dampen a cloth with straight white vinegar and wipe over tiles.

Mirrors

Put some methylated spirits into one of your spray bottles and spray onto mirrors. Use a dry soft cloth to wipe the mirrors clean. Dry with a second dry cloth or you can use a newspaper to dry and polish the mirror.

For shiny, clear mirrors and no more fog, simply wipe over mirrors with shaving cream and then polish off with a soft cloth or polish with a cloth dipped in Gumption and dry off well.

Towels

Hems on towels or hand towels have a habit of unravelling while the towel is still in good condition. Run the raw edge through the overlocker or zigzag then rehem. Once your towels look too shaggy to use, cut them into smaller face washer-sized squares and hem. Use these to remove make-up, mop up spills, as spare face washers, nappy wipes or dusting and polishing cloths.

The Laundry

One of the best and easiest ways to save money in the laundry is to use your clothes line: the heat from the sun and strength of the wind are free and together they combine to be the most efficient clothes dryer in the world.

Washing

The average family washes $70–$120 of washing powder down the drain every year. They choose expensive brands because of persuasive TV campaigns. If you must buy washing detergent, then buy in bulk and save. The larger discount retailers have 10-kilogram boxes for less than $50. This should last nearly one year and is 30 per cent cheaper than buying 1-kilogram boxes.

If you use the Cheapskate washing powder you can save around $100 per year. It is heavy-duty and costs about 3 cents per load. Make an ice-cream container full of washing powder for around $3 worth of ingredients. You will need to use about 1 tablespoon for each load to keep your clothes clean and smelling fresh. You can use even less for clothes that aren't really dirty, but just needing freshening up, such as bath towels and sheets that have been stored in the linen press for some time.

Never leave the washing machine or dryer running when you are not home. A washing machine leak or short circuit can cause water damage to floors, or even worse, start a fire.

If getting dirty clothes to the laundry is a problem in your home, try giving everyone a laundry hamper and a washing day. If their hamper is empty, don't wash on that day. Trust me, they'll only miss one or two washdays—most of us don't own enough clothes to go longer than ten days or so without running out.

Use cold water, it costs about $1 per load to heat the water. Furthermore, using hot water will tend to fade brightly coloured clothes.

Keep the water level at high—clothes need water as well as detergent to come out of the machine clean. High levels will not only clean the clothes better, they will rinse the detergents out—and many commercial washing powders irritate sensitive skin, especially in children.

Do full loads; don't waste electricity and water doing half loads.

Don't overload your washing machine; your clothes won't be cleaned or rinsed properly and you will wear out your machine, which will incur service and repair costs, or you'll need a new washing machine years earlier than necessary.

To remove stains from coloured polyester clothes, pre-soak for a few hours in a bucket of hot water in which a ¼ cup of dishwasher detergent has been dissolved, then wash as usual.

Wash bathmats in cool water as hot water causes the rubber backing to perish and peel off. Line-dry, but if you think it needs fluffing after it's dry, put it in the dryer on the coolest setting for five minutes.

Use cheap shampoo on cuffs and collars to remove stains—it works like a charm. Make the shampoo go even further by pouring a small amount into a plastic cup and using a paintbrush to paint it onto the stain. This avoids waste and you get the shampoo exactly where you want it.

If the sock fairy lives in your washing machine, keep a packet of safety pins in the laundry. As you sort the socks, pin them in pairs. This saves heaps of time when it comes to sorting the washing. Go one step further and put a packet of safety pins on everyone's dressing table. Now they are responsible for pinning the socks before they go into the wash. When the socks are dry, return the pinned socks and they can unpin them when they are going to be worn.

Instead of using expensive fabric softeners, pour ¼ cup of white vinegar into the final rinse cycle. This eliminates static cling, removes wrinkles, cleans inside the washing machine and drains and gives your clothes a clean, fresh smell by removing all traces of soap from the fabric.

Clean the lint filter on the clothes dryer after each load. And don't forget the filter in the door of some older dryers. This is hard to clean, but a quick go-over with the vacuum cleaner every couple of weeks will keep it clean.

Cut your ironing time by hanging out your washing carefully. It may take you a few minutes longer, but you won't be standing at the ironing board, slaving over a hot iron for hours on end.

Hang drip-dry garments on coathangers, hang the hook on the clothes line and when the garment is dry, place in the wardrobe.

Increase ironing efficiency by placing heavy-duty aluminium foil between your ironing board cover and pad. The foil reflects the heat and makes ironing quicker.

Wax your iron to make ironing easier: save those candle ends in an old sock and every so often, wipe the sole of your iron with it when you are ironing. The wax makes the iron glide more smoothly over clothes and helps to cut your ironing time.

Remove permanent creases with white vinegar when rehemming pants or skirts. Simply dampen with vinegar and press with a warm iron. Repeat if necessary.

Don't waste money on fabric sprays if you must use them when you iron. Simply buy a spray bottle from a two-dollar shop and fill with warm water. Spray the clothes to be ironed two or three hours before ironing to give them time to absorb the moisture and to make ironing easier.

To remove scorch marks, press a cloth dipped in 2 per cent peroxide over the stain. Repeat if necessary.

The Kitchen

Stoves and ovens

To clean dirty, greasy stoves make a thick paste of bicarb soda and water. Dip a cloth or strong paper towel into the paste and rub the grease away. Rinse with a clean cloth. Your stove will shine like new. Works much better than spray cleaners and is much, much cheaper.

Oven Cleaner

3 parts bicarb soda
1 part water
nylon scouring pad

Combine bicarb soda and water to form a paste. Spread over oven surfaces and scrub with the scouring pad using lots of elbow grease. For really stuck-on stuff, instead of three parts bicarb soda, mix half bicarb soda and half salt (this increases abrasiveness). Keep bicarb soda away from heating elements.

Sinks

For stainless steel sinks, wipe with a cloth dampened with soda water or white vinegar and dry with a soft cloth. To deep-clean, wipe with a solution of cloudy ammonia and water or dishwashing detergent and water. Dry thoroughly with a soft cloth. For porcelain sinks and basins, wipe over with a cloth soaked in undiluted white vinegar and then rinse.

Benches

Have you ever had trouble getting marks off walls, tiles, stove tops or scum off the bath? Well, look no further; I have been introduced to Gumption. It costs around $2.80 in the supermarket and it removes anything.

Cupboards

Buy sugar soap, water it down in a spray bottle and you'll be surprised at how far it goes, how quickly it cleans and how you'll be forking out for cleaning agents less often.

Chopping boards
Timber

To clean a wooden chopping board, sprinkle a handful of salt over the board and scrub the salt into the board with a half a lemon. The salt acts as an abrasive and the lemon dissolves grease. Rinse off with cold (not hot) water and dry immediately. Do not soak the board in water, just rinse and dry.

Plastic

Plastic chopping boards can be cleaned and deodorised by sprinkling with bicarb soda and scrubbing with a nylon scourer.

Appliances

If you wipe appliances regularly with a damp cloth or sponge, most will require little additional maintenance.

Lime stain on jugs

The inside of your kettle or plastic jug can show badly discoloured stains. Clean the inside of your jug using a Steradent denture tablet. Ensure that you rinse the jug thoroughly after cleaning.

The Bedroom

Beds

You'll get a better night's sleep and your mattress will last longer if you take care of it. Strip bed linen and while it's being laundered, thoroughly vacuum the mattress. Vacuum the base and then rotate and flip the mattress. (Please note: some new pillow mattresses do not need to be rotated or turned over.)

Doonas/blankets

Freshen quilts and doonas between washes by hanging them over the clothes line on a hot, sunny day. Shake them well and turn them during the day to allow the sun to reach both sides. Airing your quilts and doonas in this way will help to keep dust mites and other nasties at bay.

Wash your blankets or synthetic doonas according to the manufacturer's instructions at least once a year, preferably twice. Do not dry them in the clothes dryer but put them on the line, turning every couple of hours until completely dry. If you choose a windy day, they will become soft and fluffy, ready to go into storage for the summer or back onto the bed for winter warmth. See page 76 for a terrific Blanket and Doona Wash Recipe.

Do not wash feather or feather/down doonas. Professional dry cleaning will ensure they have a long life. In between cleans, air your feather doonas as you would for your other quilts and blankets.

Wardrobes

Clean your wardrobe from top to bottom at least once a year to deter moths, silverfish and other damaging pests. Empty wardrobe completely, then, using a soft-bristled brush or broom, sweep the top and corners to remove dust and cobwebs. Wipe shelves over with a damp cloth and white vinegar and allow to dry thoroughly. Vacuum floors, paying particular attention to corners, and clean mirrors. See pages 82 and 93 for streak-free cleaning.

Keep your wardrobes smelling fresh and clean with lavender sachets. Place them in drawers and linen cupboards, in boxes of stored clothing, blankets, etc. to keep them smelling sweet and fresh. Lavender sachets are expensive to buy, but you can make fresh ones every year if you grow your own lavender in a pot—and they make a lovely decorative feature in your garden. Collect the flowers each year to use in your sachets.

To make your own moisture absorber, fill a large empty coffee can with charcoal. (You can buy charcoal from garden stores or supermarkets in the barbecue section.) Punch some holes in the lid and put it on your wardrobe floor. For larger wardrobes or walk-in robes, use two or three coffee cans.

Lampshades

A soft natural-bristle paintbrush works wonders on lampshades. Be sure never to use this brush for any other purpose. Always brush from the top to the bottom of the shade. A weekly dusting will keep your lampshades looking brand-new for years and years.

Floors

Carpets

Regular vacuuming helps to keep carpets in tiptop shape.

Encourage your family to get into the habit of taking their shoes off before they come inside. It will save so much dirt being tracked onto your expensive floor coverings.

 An essential item in my cleaning cupboard is powdered borax. I have saved our carpet from stains a number of times using this product. We have had red wine, red grape juice, smelly carnation water, etc. spilt on our carpet. Each time there's a spill, mop up the excess moisture with a cloth then sprinkle over borax. Leave until dry, then vacuum up. Once vacuumed you wouldn't even know there had been a spill.

To get fleas out of carpet, put some chopped-up mint into a bucket of boiling water and leave to steep for a few minutes. Dip a broom into the water, shake off excess and sweep over your carpet. This will bring any fleas to the surface. Either wipe them up with a cloth dipped in kerosene, which kills them, or vacuum and throw out the vacuum bag, if your vacuum cleaner uses one.

Polished wooden floors

Sweep or vacuum floors to remove any dirt or grit that will scratch the surface. Using an almost dry mop wrung out in a solution of ½ cup methylated spirits in 4.5 litres of cold water, quickly wipe over the floors, drying as you go. Water is the enemy of timber floors, so never wet-mop and always dry off as quickly as possible when cleaning.

Tiles

1 cup of white vinegar in a bucket of hot water will hygienically clean your tiled floors in one go. There's no need to rinse, just mop and let the floor air-dry. The vinegar not only cleans, it helps to prevent spots and streaks on the tiles, too. Perfect for those fashionable high-gloss finishes.

Vinyl

Sweep or vacuum your vinyl floor. Combine 1 cup of white vinegar with a bucket of hot water and then slop the water over the vinyl. Let it sit for about five minutes and then mop. Your floor will gleam. The white vinegar brings out the shine on no-wax floors that have dulled over time and on waxed floors it helps cut through years of wax build-up, leaving the surface bright.

Slate

Vacuum or sweep the slate and clean with warm water only. Prevention is essential with this type of floor surface: regularly apply a sealant (found in tile stores) and clean up spills immediately.

Cobwebs

Take a soft-bristled broom, cover it with an old stocking and use it to knock down/sweep off the cobwebs. The cobwebs will stick to the nylon and you can just peel it off and throw it away without touching the cobwebs.

Using your homemade Swiffer cloth, put some cleaner and water in a spray bottle and use this to 'dry wash' your floors. Then when you're done, undo the face washer and drop it in the wash, ready for next time.

Windows

Streak-free clean windows

Windows also come up streak-free if you spray them with vinegar and water and squeegee over them. You can get a squeegee for a couple of dollars. Use it to clean mirrors, glass cabinet doors and car windows.

Kitchen windows

Clean greasy kitchen windows with a solution of methylated spirits and water. Spray on and wipe off with scrunched-up newspaper for sparkling-clean windows. Tip: Wipe horizontally on the inside and vertically on the outside so you can see any places you've missed.

Venetian blinds

Use your Swiffer broom to give your Venetians a clean. Close the blinds one way and, using your Swiffer broom, give them a good rub, then reverse the direction of the blind and repeat the sweeping. Attach the Swiffer to a smaller brush to get into the corners and string area. Repeat regularly for best results.

Vertical blinds

Remove the bottom chain and plates. Take the blinds off the top hooks. Place the blinds on top of each other as you remove each one. Place the blinds in the washing machine. Check with the supplier for special wash instructions. Most can either be soaked in a tub of hot soapy water or placed in a washing machine. Do not overload the machine and use the delicate cycle to avoid fraying the fabric. Hang blinds out on a clothes line to dry immediately after the load finishes or when you have completed soaking them.

Curtains

Soak dirty curtains in plenty of lukewarm water overnight before washing. A major part of the dirt will come out and an ordinary wash next morning should be sufficient.

Air Fresheners

Spice up your kitchen

Sprinkle cinnamon on aluminium foil and place it in a hot oven, leaving the door open. As the cinnamon heats, the aroma will permeate the house. Heat for 15–20 minutes, longer if necessary.

Lemon freshness

A great way to get rid of odours in your house is to leave a couple of lemons that have been cut in half on the kitchen bench. By morning the stale smell will have gone.

Absorb odours

A cup of white vinegar in a bowl will absorb odours in the air. Leave overnight to remove musty, smoky or stale odours. Use this in a sick room to get rid of the smell of vomit, too.

Pest Control

Moths and silverfish

Keep moths and silverfish at bay with mint-scented cotton balls. Simply place 3–4 drops of essential peppermint oil on cotton balls and scatter them on shelves and in drawers. Moths, silverfish, beetles, flies and even mice are repelled by mint. Refresh the cotton balls weekly with another couple of drops of oil.

Ants

Spread some ground cinnamon where you think the ants are coming into the house. To deter ants, sprinkle catnip on their paths.

Ant Deterrent

⅔ cup water
⅓ cup white vinegar
2–3 tablespoons dishwashing detergent

Combine water, vinegar and detergent and mix well. Spray where the ants are marching.

Mosquitoes and ticks

Splashing plain rubbing alcohol on yourself and allowing it to dry will deter mosquitoes from biting you.

Rub Vicks VapoRub on your jeans or trousers and legs to ward off ticks.

Use equal quantities of vanilla essence and water for a mosquito and tick repellent. Spray this on using a recycled mist spray bottle.

Insect repellent

Dab lavender oil on your pulse points; it smells great on you and repels insects.

Mice, birds and bugs

Place used kitty litter from a litter box in small tubs in places where mice may be a problem. Mice think ... it smells like a cat ... must be a cat ... I'm outta here!

Mice hate the scent of peppermint. Simply sprinkle peppermint oil on the items you don't want mice in or on.

To prevent mice from gaining entry in the first place, stop up any openings, especially around plumbing, vents, etc. with steel wool pads. Mice will not chew through these!

Buy a mesh/net laundry bag that you would use for washing delicates and a box of mothballs. Put the mothballs in the bag and hang it in your garage near the door to get rid of mice, birds and bugs.

Sprinkle cayenne pepper around the garage (inside and out) and especially near entry holes. Pests don't care for the smell of it.

Lice

Head lice are an inevitable part of going to school. They are so contagious that most children get them at some point no matter how clean their hair. There are a number of Cheapskate ways to treat lice that are environmentally friendly and minimise health concerns. There is no single lice treatment that is guaranteed to kill them the first time. You may need to reapply these treatments more than once, so choose the one that suits your needs. Victorian Schools recommend KP24, this is $12.95 for 100-millilitre bottle. It's a chemical treatment, and carries a health and usage warning. Here are some options that will remove nits and are inexpensive and safe.

Hair conditioner

Use the cheapest conditioner you can find—$2 a litre from the local discount shop. Cover dry hair with a thick layer of conditioner, rub through and then cover with a shower cap. The shower cap isn't necessary, but it keeps the conditioner out of eyes and off clothing and furniture. Leave for at least 30 minutes, then sit with a towel across your lap with the child in front of you. Use a fine-toothed comb to comb every strand of hair, wiping the conditioner on the towel after every stroke. When you have combed the hair thoroughly, shampoo and condition as usual. Repeat this treatment every second day until there are no head lice found for at least ten consecutive days.

Tea-tree shampoo and conditioner

Buy some tea-tree shampoo and conditioner to repel lice. They are quite expensive: $4.70 for a 200-millilitre bottle of Thursday Island

Tea Tree Shampoo and the same for the conditioner. It will cost approximately 94 cents a treatment. While it is a healthier option than many of the chemical-laden commercial lice products, it is still quite expensive, especially if you have two or more children and need to apply it yearly.

Tea-tree oil
Buy a bottle of pure tea-tree oil; a 10-millilitre bottle costs approximately $3.60. Add one or two drops to your regular shampoo and conditioner. A bottle of tea-tree oil lasts for a very long time.

Tea-tree spray
Make up a spray of 1 part tea-tree oil to 10 parts water and use it as a hair spray each day to help deter lice and to repel any that are present. This mixture is strong enough to work without burning or irritating a little scalp.

Vinegar
Vinegar breaks down the sticky substance that glues the nits to the strands of hair—and lice don't like vinegar. Use white vinegar as a rinse after shampooing, then comb hair with a lice comb or add a splash of vinegar to a spray bottle of water and use as hair spray every morning after hair has been done.

Boil hair accessories
Boil brushes, combs, hair clips and hair ties, etc. for at least thirty minutes to kill any lice or nits that are caught in them. Doing this religiously every week will help to control any further outbreaks.

Lice generally live for only 6–24 hours once they are off the human scalp, but eggs take up to ten days to hatch and if they hatch in a hairbrush and then get lucky and are put straight onto a nice, clean head the cycle will continue.

Weekly head checks

It might seem like a waste of time, but a weekly check of heads and hair is essential in keeping head lice and nits at bay. It only takes a few minutes to go over a child's head. If you find any evidence of lice or nits, you can start a treatment routine immediately and keep something that can quite easily become an epidemic under control, eventually stamping it out.

Eating

Eating Well and Saving Money

The average family spends about 15 per cent of its total income on food. That is a huge portion of the total amount of money that comes into your home each week. If your income is a total of $40,000 per year, that means you are likely to be spending $6000 a year on food. If you earn $60,000 or $100,000 per year then you are likely to be spending $9000 or $15,000 respectively on food bills. Imagine what you could do with, say, 20 per cent or 30 per cent of the money you are spending on food. In a household with an income of $40,000, if you could shave 25 per cent off your food bill, you would have an extra $1500 a year to use as extra payments on your mortgage, which would shave as much as six months off the length of your loan. For a household with an income of $100,000, shaving 20 per cent off your food bill of $15,000 would give you an extra $3000 a year. That would pay for a great family holiday or could be used to renovate the back garden.

Your grocery bill is one of the most flexible items in the family budget, so let's look at the Cheapskate way to eating well and saving money.

Let's start by stating up front that being a Cheapskate means buying the groceries that you need to prepare tasty, nutritious and good-value food at the cheapest price. This does not mean buying rubbish food because it's cheap, rather it is about buying efficiently—shopping, cooking and saving the smart way.

The average family cook serves about twenty-two different meals. These include the usual family favourites, such as spaghetti

Bolognese, hamburgers, casseroles, roasts, meat with three veg and so on. While most people will experiment with an average of one new recipe each month, our shopping lists stay relatively standard.

Smart shopping

Minimise the number of trips you make to the supermarket. Over 75 per cent of people will buy at least two or three items that they did not plan to buy with each trip to the supermarket. Shopping only once a week or even fortnightly can save you $20 per month immediately. That's $240 per year.

One study I read indicated that 50 per cent of supermarket purchases are unplanned. This can lead to forgetting to buy the items that you need and instead picking up unnecessary items, which costs you more money in the long run. You will have to return sooner to buy the things you forgot and you are likely to buy those two or three items that you didn't really need at the same time.

Set a savings budget

Think of it this way: if you can shave just $10 a week off your grocery bill you'll save $520 in a year! Many people have taken this one step further and have written to tell us that when they started shopping the Cheapskate way they saved $1000 or $2000 per year.

Menu plan

To be a Cheapskate, you need to do a quick menu plan before you go shopping. Creating a menu plan isn't hard or time-consuming: I try to think of different ways to use what I have so I won't spend too much, but I don't keep to a strict menu. Thinking about what you can make with what you have on hand saves you shopping time and you won't be throwing away good food gone bad or keeping a stockpile in the pantry for no reason. Use your junk mail to plan what you'll eat; for example, if chicken fillets are on sale, plan to have apricot chicken, chicken cacciatore and fajitas that week. You could even make chicken noodle soup. Take full advantage of the store's loss leaders—the items put on sale to entice you to shop with them rather than their competitors. Don't forget to check your price book so you know if it's a genuine bargain.

Build your meal plans around:

- What you are going to eat for the week
- What you have on hand in the fridge and pantry
- What you have to buy
- How much it is going to cost
- What is on sale this week—take a quick glance at shopping catalogues
- Fruit and vegetables that are in season—pumpkins, squash, onions, apples and potatoes are in season in winter, whereas summer has wonderful stone fruits as well as tomatoes and salad produce
- Fruit and vegetables from your garden—don't have one? Think of starting one, it is great fun for the children.

Set aside one meal a week as a mufti meal—we usually have this on a Friday or Saturday night. We finish off the leftovers and eat all the odd things left in the fridge. Some weeks we have heaps of food, whereas at other times we may need to add to it with some fried rice or pizza. Our mufti meal cleans out the fridge, reduces our food wastage and we have family fun as the kids are actively involved in the food preparation.

Smart shopping rules
Keep it simple

Keep your daily meals simple, tasty, nutritious and filling. The family will love them and you will be proud to see your family fit and healthy. If one family member particularly likes a type of gourmet or spicy food, why not make up and freeze enough for several lunches?

Get more bang for your buck!

Grocery shopping with a menu plan allows you to confidently shop and save knowing you are buying the ingredients you need to cook nutritious meals. Be mindful that supermarkets and grocery giants spend millions of dollars a year to entice you into their stores to buy high-priced processed foods that give the supermarket maximum profits. Likewise, they are always looking for ways to get you to buy more—whether you need the items or not. Knowing how to beat them at their own game, will save you hundreds of dollars and hours each year. Do this by buying more of their specials and fewer of the high-priced add-on products.

Know the store layout

Knowing the store layout can save you so much time. Plan your shopping list according to the shop layout. This will help you save time as you won't be tempted to walk down aisles from which you don't need to buy anything. Try to list your shopping in aisle order to allow you to quickly and efficiently move through the store without backtracking or criss-crossing. You will save 10–15 minutes and $10–$30 each shop by not buying things you don't need.

Look high, look low

The supermarkets effectively sell their prime shelf space, which is at eye height and slightly below. You will often find the most expensive brands or supermarket brands located here because they are easy to see and convenient for you to reach. However, the cheaper products are located on the bottom shelves where they are hard for you to see and you have to bend down to select them. Now, cheaper doesn't necessarily mean less quality; it often means the manufacturer doesn't spend as much on advertising, so their costs are lower and they can pass on their savings with a cheaper price.

Shop the perimeter

The fresh food—bakery, fruit and vegetables, meat and unprocessed food—are usually located on the perimeters of the supermarket. They require fridges or easy access for refilling. Plan to spend more time in these regions and you will save money. There is no doubt that buying fresh food is much cheaper than filling your trolley with cans or pre-packaged foods. It is very easy to shave 30 per cent off the total cost of your grocery bills simply by doing a little more cooking yourself. And eating healthier and fresher food will make you look and feel great.

Just the specials

Ensure you have a list of the specials that you need. Remember, one of the secrets is to buy only the food you need, not the food the supermarkets want you to buy. Don't get duped into buying the complementary goods they display to entice you to spend extra money.

Shop alone

Leave the family at home and shop alone. You will spend less money without the kids adding products they have seen advertised on TV and you will save time as you move through the aisles faster and buy only items you need.

Price check

Know the prices of your grocery items and watch the price displayed as it moves through the scanners. Sometimes sale items are not reduced and that will cost you money. If you are unsure of a price, ask for a price check. Know the store policy on incorrect scans—you may receive it for free.

Check stickers

Some stores still put individual price stickers on goods. As prices rise, lazy shelf packers don't always mark all products. On non-perishable items you can often find cheaper items further back on the shelf. Of course, be sure that the old price is the cheaper price.

Buy in bulk

Join a bulk-buying food co-op or start your own with five or six other families. Bulk buying can save you between 20 and 35 per cent off the retail price of your food groceries and 50 to 80 per cent on bathroom and cleaning products (see Buying in Bulk on pages 48–49).

Buy on the sales cycle

Get to know your grocery stores and discount warehouses. You will know which store is about to have particular items, such as soap powder, toilet paper, margarine or cereals, on sale. Manufacturers often reduce them in cycles so that they are on sale at a different supermarket each week.

Discount coupons

Look for discount coupons and use them to save money. You can save between 10 and 20 per cent on a variety of things by using your vouchers and coupons, which can add up to anywhere from $100 to $1000 a year if used wisely. Remember to use them only on things you need to buy.

Lunch and Snack Ideas

Cheapskates know that buying lunch can be expensive—$7 a day adds up to a whopping $1610 a year ($35 per week x 46 weeks worked)! SCARY! Now consider spending ten minutes each day and $2.50 for the cost of making lunch—you'll save at least $1035 in just one year! As a bonus you may notice that your health improves, you'll have less stress because you won't be queuing to buy food and you may even be able to cut the cost of packed lunches to $2.25 or even $2 a day.

If you think you don't have time to make lunch each day, think about making lunches ahead and freezing them—you could prepare a whole month of lunches in under an hour! Or prepare tomorrow's lunch the night before by using dinner leftovers and storing them in the fridge. Grabbing some quiche and a muffin out of the freezer and a piece of fruit from the fridge is much easier on your wallet than buying a sandwich, chocolate bar and fizzy drink at lunchtime. Most still-frozen lunchbox items will thaw by lunchtime. And as a bonus, they will keep the other contents cool and fresh, saving you the cost of buying freezer bricks.

Some quick, easy and frugal lunchbox ideas are:

Sandwiches

These can be made ahead, wrapped and frozen. Some fillings suitable to freeze are meat, tuna, salmon, hard cheeses, cream cheese, hardboiled egg yolks (the whites get rubbery), peanut butter and chocolate hazelnut spread.

Lightly butter your bread to prevent it going soggy. Adding the sauce, dressing or mayo to the filling helps to prevent soggy bread too. Avoid adding salad ingredients to sandwiches and rolls that are to be frozen as they go limp and soggy. You can always add these after you've taken them out of the freezer. To save time, set up an assembly line in the kitchen. I can make a whole month's worth of sandwiches and rolls for four people in under an hour.

Quiches

You can slice up a large quiche or make individual mini quiches (using a patty pan). Quiche can be eaten cold or hot and is a tasty substitute for sandwiches.

Soups

Make your own soup and freeze single serves in microwave-safe containers. Then it just has to be reheated at lunchtime.

Pasta dishes

These can be frozen in single-serve portions and reheated in the microwave. Some suggestions are pasta bake, spaghetti, lasagne and cannelloni.

Pancakes

These make a great alternative to bread. Fill pancakes with desired filling, wrap, freeze and they are ready to go. You can either make your own or use a bought mix. Sometimes buying a mix on sale is cheaper than making your own, so keep an eye out for sales.

Cakes, muffins, biscuits and slices

These can all be cut into individual portions, wrapped and frozen, then in the mornings it's a simple task to open the freezer and grab a dessert to go!

Dinner ideas

Good food does not mean high grocery bills. You can make great meals economically if you have just a few basic and inexpensive ingredients in the kitchen. You can grow your own herbs very cheaply and with limited space. Buy small plants or grow from seeds and plant into pots that you can use to decorate verandas or porches. Pick fresh as needed.

Always have on hand:

- Onions
- Garlic
- Celery
- Red or green capsicum
- Turnips
- Carrots
- Ground cumin
- Sage: fresh and dried
- Stock cubes: chicken, vegetable and beef
- Olive oil
- Thyme: fresh and dried
- Basil
- Oregano: fresh and dried
- Flat-leaf parsley

Part 2:

CHEAPSKATE
ways to save money

Family Fun

Preschoolers

When children are small they are cheap to amuse and little imaginations are incredibly creative. It's true what they say: give a baby a present and they'll play with the wrapping paper for hours! Babies and toddlers love playing with simple items such as boxes—putting things in and tipping them out—and the contents of the plastics cupboard—emptying out all the containers, stacking them up and knocking them down. Now, we're not saying you shouldn't have good-quality toys and games for your littlies, but we do believe that you don't need to spend a fortune on toys with bells, whistles and flashing lights. When shopping for toys, games and puzzles, just think about who you are shopping for: the child or yourself?

Messy play

Preschoolers love mess—the messier the play the happier they are. How often have you seen children having a ball playing in a puddle or covering themselves in paint? Remember, children come clean in the bath so encourage them to play and develop their creativity. If you put down a drop sheet or let them play outside then cleaning up isn't really a problem.

Finger Paint

Children love to finger-paint. It is a very messy, gooey activity. Finding cheap paper for the kids to use is easy. Butcher's paper is great or use newspaper, used office paper or ask at your local printers for overruns and wastage.

2 tablespoons sugar
⅓ cup cornflour
2 cups cold water
¼ cup dishwashing detergent
Food colouring or tempera paint

Combine sugar and cornflour in a saucepan. Slowly stir in water and cook over low heat until smooth and transparent. Remove from heat and cool. Stir in dishwashing detergent, divide between a few containers and colour each with food colour or paint.

Blocks and beads

Collect a lot of cardboard rolls—from toilet paper, paper towels, etc.—cut them into different lengths, leaving some long. Cover with bright contact paper or wrapping paper, covering over the edges a little. Using a sharp kitchen knife, make four slits about 2cm long on each end, cutting across with the knife so that they are even. Older kids can use these as blocks, interlocking the slits for stacking. Without the slits, they make great beads for the little ones to string onto a long shoelace; just watch that they don't chew on them.

Teddy bears' picnic

Children love a picnic—especially with their favourite teddy bears. Have teddy-sized food with mini cup cakes, pizzas, sausage rolls, sandwiches, etc. Play teddy bear music, and sing teddy bear songs. Have some teddy bear games like three-legged races, egg-and-spoon races and hide-and-seek. Enjoy!

Playgrounds

Take the kids to the park. They love to run, jump and play and there are some fantastic children's playgrounds and parks around. You can join in the fun or sit back and cheer them on.

Petting zoos

There are zoos around that have been set up in inner-city areas to enable children to see and interact with farm animals. They are low-cost outings and the children love patting the animals.

Baby animals

Shopping centres may have baby farm animals as an attraction during school holidays. Take them along and let them enjoy the lambs and piglets. These are normally free, so you may want to go twice to let the children get used to the animals.

Zoo and wildlife parks

These are not particularly cheap, but they are excellent fun for the children. They usually have a range of Australian wildlife as well as Asian and African favourites (the kids love the monkeys) and reptiles. Take a picnic lunch and make a day of it. (See page 128 for information on how to save a packet going to the zoo.)

Feed the birds

Children love to feed birds, whether they are ducks at a local pond, seagulls at the beach or pigeons at the park. Take some stale bread or biscuits with you. If the children are small, tear the bread or crush the biscuits into smaller pieces.

Tea parties

Children also love to play make-believe. Little ones will want you to sit and play with them drinking pretend cups of tea and eating pretend scones, while bigger ones can make (with your help) a real tea party. Try dressing up or being characters from a TV show just to add some fun and excitement to the event.

Dressing up

Children adore dressing up. Give all your old clothes, shoes, bags, hats, wraps and jewellery to the kids and keep them in a special dressing up box ready for use. The kids will play happily for hours. Have the children do a singing and dancing show or if they are older have them perform in a play. Make it fun with some popcorn and don't forget to video it for their twenty-first birthday party!

For some additional adventures, take a look at your local charity/opportunity shop for quirky and unusual clothes. You often find great dress-up clothes and shoes for $1 or $2. Look for bright and outlandish costumes and don't forget to wash the clothes before using.

Playgroups

Playgroups that consist of mums and dads who get together to let their children play once a week or so can be found almost everywhere. They have organised insurance to cover the children and are usually held at church halls, play centres, local parks and playgrounds.

Shell collecting

Summer or winter, children love going to the beach to collect shells and build sandcastles. Always take a ball, a small spade and bucket and be prepared with sunscreen, hats and a change of clothes—they love getting wet.

Toy libraries

Many communities have organised toy libraries, which are often run by volunteers. You pay a minimum amount to join and then must contribute two roster days per year to stay a member. Rather than buying expensive toys, look into hiring them from your local toy library or borrow a friend's for a week before you buy. Often the toys you think they will like they don't care for, and vice versa!

Our local toy library is packed full of toys for children of all ages. I find it invaluable as I can choose toys that complement the stages my children have reached without the expense of buying them. I have noticed that our local library also has a huge range of costumes for dress-ups and play-acting. While my young one is too little for this right now, I know it will save me a fortune later.

Bubble fun

Bubbles have long been a traditional warm-weather fun activity for kids. Buy a couple of plastic implements with holes in them and blow bubbles until the air is filled and the kids are laughing!

Bubble Mixture

If you have hard water use bottled distilled water instead of tap water.

1 part dishwashing detergent
10 parts water
25 parts glycerine

Combine ingredients and store in a covered container.

Cardboard box

A cardboard box can be a cubbyhouse, boat, car, bus or plane—the list is almost endless. Ask your local grocer to keep a sturdy carton or two for you and let your kids use their imagination. A larger box, such as a refrigerator carton, can become a tower for a princess or an apartment building for dolls; it can be a fire-engine one day and a spaceship the next. If you want it to be a lasting toy, you can easily paint and decorate it with stickers or pictures cut out of magazines and glued on. If you use small sample paint pots for the paint job, you may not even have to pay for them.

Big blackboards

Here's a fun idea for a kids' room. Section off part of a wall, frame it with mouldings and paint it with chalkboard paint. You can make it as big as you want and your kids will be able to write on the wall— which they will love! You can also do this on a door or a piece of furniture.

Learning books

Use a small photo album with a bright, colourful cover to make a beginner book for your baby or toddler. Insert photos of baby, Mum, Dad, grandparents, siblings and pets and let your baby 'read' the pictures.

Older Children

There are many things that you can do with your kids that don't cost large sums of money. Rather than simply turning on the TV or paying for the kids to go to the movies, look for activities that you can do together that won't cost a thing.

Board games

Scrabble, Monopoly, and Snakes and Ladders are all expensive to buy brand new. Keep a lookout in your local paper for garage sales where you'll get great bargains. I picked up a brand-new, unopened Scrabble set for just $8 at a garage sale. It went into the present box as we already had Scrabble and Junior Scrabble.

Crafty ideas

Crystal Garden

Crystal gardens are a fun educational activity. They are very pretty, but are quite fragile. Put the dish where it is going to stay before the crystals start to grow as moving it will cause the crystals to crumble.

several charcoal briquettes
6 tablespoons salt
6 tablespoons liquid bluing*
6 tablespoons water
1 tablespoon clear ammonia
liquid food colouring

Arrange charcoal in a glass bowl or pie plate. Combine salt, liquid bluing, water and ammonia in another bowl and pour over charcoal. Drop various colours of food colouring over charcoal. Crystals will begin to grow all over the charcoal and will continue to grow for several days, changing every day.

*You can find this in a small blue bottle in the laundry section of the supermarket; it is used instead of bleach to keep whites really white.

Candle Holder

diluted PVA glue
baby-food jar
tissue paper
glitter
ribbons
small votive candle

Brush glue on the outside of the jar and cover the whole jar with one layer of tissue paper. Sprinkle a little glitter on it, and tie a ribbon around the top if you like. Place candle inside and use.

Playdough

All kids love playdough, even the big ones. It's very simple and extremely cheap to make and lasts for ages. It is a great party favourite, too! Save your takeaway containers to store it in. These can be personalised with each child's name and the date of the birthday party, all ready for them to take home.

1 cup plain flour
¼ cup salt
1 tablespoon vegetable oil
a few drops of food colouring
½ cup boiling water

Combine ingredients in a bowl and knead to form a dough consistency. Place in an airtight container.

Flubber

This is such fun to make and even more fun to play with.

1 cup PVA glue
1½ cups cold water
food colouring
1⅓ cups boiling water
2 teaspoons borax

Dilute glue with a small amount of cold water in a bowl. Add some food colouring and, mixing well, carefully add boiling water and borax, a little at a time, until it is thick and resembles playdough. Turn out and knead well. Then go and have some fun with your flubber!

Cable cars

To make a tram or cable car set-up, cut 5 centimetres off the end of a straw and stick it along the side of a toilet paper roll with glue or sticky tape. Get your child to decorate the rolls with crayons or Textas and draw windows, doors and faces for the passengers. Feed a length of string or wool through the straw. Tie both ends of the string to the backs of chairs, making sure that one end of the string is higher than the other and that the string is taut. Place a piece of playdough or Blu-Tack inside the roll to give it some weight. Move the tube to the high point, and then let it slide down. Let the kids make one each and they can have races!

Old-fashioned games

These are great for a really hot day, when kids can't play outside or on those really long and boring wet days.

Teach the kids to play:

- Dominoes
- Old Maid
- Snap
- Draughts
- Charades—they love acting out the answers to this one
- Monopoly
- Scrabble.

Try playing a marathon with any or all of these games.

Nature walk journal

Give the children a notebook, a pencil and a small magnifying glass and they can walk around the garden looking closely at plants, rocks and other objects. Tell them to record what they see, where they found it and why it is interesting. Have a show-and-tell of what was found. You can do this again next week and see what has changed. Keep the notebooks so the children can check and compare as the seasons change.

Catch public transport

Children love to ride in buses, trains and trams looking at all the traffic and people coming in and out. Take a ride to the local beach, bay, river or go into town. Take a backpack with a drink and snack for the ride and your lunch for when you arrive.

 One of our favourite family fun days so far has been playing tourist in the city. We collected maps and guides and did a walking tour of the city. We found places and things we didn't even know existed and had an absolute ball at the same time.

Walking

There are so many beautiful places to take the kids for walks. Count all the different flowers or look for birds, sing some children's songs together and talk with your children as you go.

Barbecues

Wonderful public barbecue areas are popping up everywhere. Many councils have upgraded the tired and often dangerous wood-burning barbecues for clean and efficient gas ones. While some will charge to use them, many are free.

We have a local park about 2 kilometres away that has a wonderful playground for children, a picnic table and a barbecue area. We often bundle the kids into the car and head for the park where they play for an hour or so until they are thirsty and hungry and then we have a barbecue or a picnic. We clean up and enjoy chatting to each other while the children run around and burn off excess energy. When we leave, there is always a chorus of can't we stay longer, yet they are always in bed and fast asleep within an hour of being home. The best thing is that it is free to use the playground equipment, picnic area and barbecue. Dinner is simple with no mess to clean up at the end—just a few plates to throw into the dishwasher.

For a barbecue, take sausages, bread and tomato ketchup and maybe some eggs. Make a pocket salad by wrapping a lettuce leaf around some finely chopped salad vegetables. Finish with a piece of fresh fruit. For a picnic, hardboiled eggs with a funny face drawn on the shell can be a winner. Teach older children how to peel the egg and eat it. Give them a wholemeal roll with a tasty filling and finish with fresh fruit.

Picnics

Take the children and a picnic brunch/lunch/dinner and head for a local park or beach. The kids will be kept busy playing and running around.

Popstars

Encourage your children to put on a concert. They can be their favourite popstar or TV personality. Make a singing set using some old sheets or have the children make a colourful set using a cardboard box. Remember the video!

Theme trails

Take a journey around your local area or city following a theme. You might be walking in the footsteps of ... or visiting historic sites. Consider following a sporting theme, pop or movie-star theme. Use public transport and you can have a ball going all over town looking at the sights.

Botanic gardens

Take the children to your local botanic gardens. They have such a wonderful array of plants and flowers. Encourage the kids to choose their favourite flower or spot the most unusual shaped leaf. You can walk along the various paths and they have lovely grassy areas to sit for a snack or picnic.

Stop and smell the roses

As adults we use the phrase, so why not teach the children how to appreciate the fragrance of various flowers and plants. Encourage them to smell and learn the names of the flowers, but discourage them from picking them. Look for butterflies, ladybugs and local insects while walking.

Trekking
Take the family for a drive to a local national park or mountain range, follow well-marked tracks to the top of the mountain and teach the children to appreciate the spectacular view. Always be well prepared—your local national or state park rangers can help you with information, conditions and preparations to make.

Rent a movie
Children love watching classic movies like *Mary Poppins*, *Chitty Chitty Bang Bang*, *Bedknobs and Broomsticks* and *Benji* when they are young. As these are old movies you can hire them more cheaply. Make some popcorn and sit down with the kids for a walk down memory lane.

Local library
The library is a great resource for children of all ages. They have children's storytelling sessions for free and it is a terrific place for children to sit and read. You can enjoy a few of the latest magazines for free as well.

Read a good book
On a wet winter day there is nothing like curling up on the couch and reading a good book. Teach your children from a young age to enjoy the same pleasures. They can visit far-away countries exploring lost and forgotten lands, solve mysteries or read about cute teddy bears' picnics.

Make hot chocolate and pop some popcorn

Children love popcorn and if you cut back on the salt and butter, it is a healthy snack. Teach them how to make it from scratch on the stove or buy a cheap popping machine. Make some hot chocolate and enjoy some time together chatting.

Bake biscuits

Bake some biscuits with the children. Have a competition to make shapes ready for baking or to decorate the biscuits when they have cooled.

Games night

Have a games night with the children. Choose the games to suit, set up a play table and have some refreshments ready. Have a piece of butcher's paper for the scoring and have little prizes for the winners. Mix up the teams to ensure everyone is a winner.

Card games

Play Snap or Fish with younger children, and for older kids buy a card game, such as Skip-Bo or Uno. Children can have hours of fun playing cards and they are great for holiday entertainment. A book of card games is a worthwhile investment or good to borrow from the library.

Backyard fun

Make a picnic lunch and head to the backyard. Put down a blanket and enjoy the picnic. Use your imagination to create a story about a flying carpet and far-away lands or play with the dog or read a book and enjoy the sunshine.

Free children's activities

Your local council, shopping centre, library, charity groups and schools may offer free children's activities, such as concerts, dance groups or outdoor fun. Keep your eye on the local papers, children's newspapers and magazines for details and take advantage of the fun and new experiences they offer.

Pool party

Invite a neighbour's child, a school friend or a playgroup pal for a BYO pool party: they bring their own drinks and food and you supply the pool. Whether it's a big pool or just a wading pool, children will love it on a hot day.

Kite flying

Buy a cheap kite or make your own from a plastic bag and paper rolls. Find a local park away from power lines and cables to fly the kite. Remember, children like to see the kite flying up and down. It is the grown-up kids (dads) who need it to reach flight-path levels and be a masterpiece of aerodynamics.

Ice-cream

Drive to a local ice-creamery and buy the children an ice-cream for a treat after they have had a walk in the park. Look for kiddie cones for small children—they are easier to manage and are a more friendly size to eat.

Free local attractions

Many towns and cities have free tourist activities, so join in the fun. In Melbourne, they have a free city-circuit tram and a free tourist bus. Each ride takes over an hour to complete and if you jump on and off at some of the sights, such as churches or parks, you could spend a whole day having fun.

Keep a straight face

Two teams sit facing each other in two lines. One team is chosen to go first and they must keep a straight face no matter what. In the meantime, the opposing team is doing everything within their power to make the other team laugh or crack a smile. There is no touching or tickling, but other than that, anything goes! It's so funny to watch the creative ways people try to make each other laugh.

Spot the thimble

Everyone leaves the room for a moment while one person hides a thimble somewhere in plain sight in the room. When the people who left the room return, as soon as each person sees the thimble they sit down without letting others know where the thimble is hiding. The last one to find the thimble does a forfeit dance of some sort. They might have to sing a song, recite a poem, spell their name backwards, kiss their own shadow, etc. The first one to see the thimble hides it on the next round.

Internet information

Use the internet to find discount vouchers for meals, movies, accommodation, etc. when you are planning a trip. Whether it's a day trip, a weekend away or a family holiday, you are sure to find plenty of bonus offers or last-minute deals online.

We use the Internet to scout around for discount coupons and vouchers for weekends away and holidays. We've found accommodation with free meals and we've discovered that memberships we have make us eligible for discounts. Many companies use the internet to take direct bookings so they pass on bonuses to people booking that way.

Saturday-night movie

Make Saturday night stay-at-home-pizza-and-movie night. You can pick up movies quite cheaply using discount vouchers or taking advantage of weekly specials. Make your own tasty pizza with the children's favourite toppings and you are set for a great night in. Don't forget to make your own popcorn.

Make fantastic pizzas by using Lebanese bread as your base. Top with tomato paste, olives, capsicum, cheese, pineapple, mushrooms and any leftover meat cut up into chunks. Pizzas only take 5 minutes in the oven at 220°C/425°F and as the kids get older they can be creative and add their own toppings.

Cheap movie tickets

You can get cheap movie tickets from the smaller independent cinemas. If you don't have an independent close by, check out the websites of the larger chains; they often have special sessions that are cheaper.

Super Savings Hint: *The Village cinema at the Waverley Gardens shopping centre in Melbourne, for example, has $5.50 movie tickets to all movies, all sessions, all day, every day. They even have a movie club you can join for further discounts. If you love the cinema experience it's worth a few minutes to do some research and find cheaper tickets.*

Family memberships

Many attractions have family memberships; for example, galleries, museums, science centres—the CSIRO has yearly passes—and most zoos offer a yearly membership. This one-off fee allows admission all year.

We have had a museum membership since our boys were little. It gets us into the museum and its annexes, and with reciprocal deals we can get free admission to interstate museums, too. The annual membership is just a few dollars more than the cost of one family visit to the museum. As this is something we do at least four times a year, we are way out in front.

Zoo memberships work in a similar way to the museum memberships. If you are regular visitors or plan to become regular visitors then a membership is worth looking into. Check the reciprocal arrangements with other zoos around the country and the special events that are only available to members.

We became Friends of the Zoo this year and within two months had our money's worth. As we have younger children, we go to the zoo for a couple of hours at a time, often during the week when there are fewer people. It is great to be able to go for shorter periods more frequently, as the children get maximum benefit from the experience. There are two zoos in Melbourne (Melbourne Zoo and Healesville Sanctuary) that we alternate between as they have totally different set-ups and animals. We have free entry into most of the other zoos around Australia and we are planning to see an interstate zoo on our next holiday. It is a wonderful program and I encourage others to use it. Also, they send out a free magazine four times a year with terrific pictures of the animals. We cut them out and put them into a scrapbook for our little one to look at.

Entertainment books

These books cost around $60 and have vouchers for between 10 per cent and 50 per cent off the price of restaurant meals, takeaway, dry-cleaning, video rental, car wash, accommodation, beauty, etc. As the book costs you money, make sure the vouchers are for things you are going to buy; don't buy it just to use a single voucher.

My children's school uses Entertainment Books as a fundraiser. We buy one each year and find we use a lot of the vouchers. The books have discounts available in Adelaide, Brisbane, the Sunshine and Gold coasts, Canberra, Central Coast, Newcastle, Hunter Valley, Melbourne, Sydney, Perth and more areas. Vouchers are valid from June 1 to June 1 the following year.

Babies and Children

To some people, having a baby means spending thousands of dollars on new furniture, baby clothes, toys and decorations. The Cheapskate way costs less than a few hundred dollars. Rather than buying everything brand-new and paying full price, think about creative ways to clothe the children, fit out their rooms and buy toys. Before you go and spend up big, talk to your friends and family as they may have items from when their children were small that they would love to give or lend to you. As your child grows older, suggest ideas to family and friends for Christmas and birthday presents—this helps to avoid getting those interesting gifts that are never really appreciated.

Shopping Strategies

Look in the *Trading Post*, the local paper, on eBay and at garage sales for baby essentials. You will find that often they are in perfectly good condition and people are happy to sell them cheaply because they want them to go to nice homes. Remember to ask other mums at mothers' group or your playgroup. They could be looking to sell 'outgrown' baby goods or might be able to tell you where to get the best deals.

Super Savings Hint: *I shopped around and looked in the local paper and at garage sales for our pram and stroller. I got great deals on both. Our $400 pram we bought for just $80 and our $100 stroller was just $20. We used them for all three children and then passed them on.*

Think second-hand

Wherever possible borrow or buy second-hand baby furniture and clothes. A second-hand cot can cost as little as $50 with $10 for some fresh paint whereas a new cot can cost anywhere from $400 to over $1000. A cradle can be hired for around $40 a month (you only need it for two months) and clothes can be as cheap as $1.

 We didn't have to buy very much at all new for any of our babies. We were given more than we could possibly use, including furniture, toys and clothes. What we weren't given we bought from garage sales or op shops. If we couldn't buy it, we made it. I had three nappy buckets with tight-fitting lids and they didn't cost a cent. They were recycled from an ice-cream shop. The manager was more than happy to give them to me; all I did was ask. Borrow things that you are going to use for only a short time. Our cradle was borrowed from a friend. We did buy a new tea-tree mattress for it and once AJ had grown out of the cradle we returned it, but we kept the mattress for the next baby.

Buy direct

Buy your nursery furniture directly from the manufacturer or importer. You may save up to 50 per cent on the retail price—the middle man adds 100 per cent to the price of the item. You will find manufacturers and importers advertising in local papers, Yellow Pages or the *Trading Post*. Be prepared to do a deal.

> **Super Savings Hint:** *We bought our cot straight from the manufacturer and saved $200 off the cheapest retail price we had seen. For the mattress, we rang around and found a mattress manufacturer who would sell direct for cash. We saved 50 per cent off the RRP.*

Buy unpainted furniture

If you are buying furniture from the manufacturer, consider getting it delivered unpainted or unstained. You will save more money and be able to decorate it to match other items in the room.

> **Super Savings Hint:** *My parents bought a new chest of unpainted drawers for our baby. Dad picked up our second-hand cot and gave it a quick sand and then painted the cot and drawers the same colour—they looked terrific when finished.*

Markets and trash and treasure

You can pick up great kids' clothes at your local market. You may pay as little as $1–$5 for top labels for which you would normally pay $25–$50.

Trade or swap clothes

Swap clothes with family, friends or neighbours who have children of a similar size to yours. This is a great way to avoid the siblings' hand-me-downs: the kids get a new look and the price is right.

Opportunity/charity shops

Op shops and charity stores are terrific for buying good-quality kids' clothes. They won't stock rubbish, worn or tatty clothes and the prices are very reasonable. Go to two or three shops and find one that stocks children's brands you like to buy.

Buy on sale

If you choose to buy from major chain or department stores, wait for the sales. Competition between them is tight and they all have 15–40 per cent off clothes and toys at different times of the year. On a $30 item you save $6 in a 20 per cent-off sale.

Cut down adult versions

Some baby products are overpriced. Buy a queen-sized mattress protector (for less than the price of one baby protector), cut it down and you can make three cot-sized mattress protectors.

Cradle or cot

If your cot has an adjustable base that will allow you to set it high enough so you don't need to bend over in the early months, you may not need a cradle. Shortsheet the cot and put the baby straight into a cot. To shortsheet the cot, fold the top sheet in such a way that the baby's feet are placed at the base of the cot so that he or she can't slide under the sheets.

Multipurpose furniture

Lift the base of the cot and use the mattress as a change table until the baby has grown out of the cradle. You'll have plenty of space and with the rail up the baby won't be able to roll off. Another idea is to use the top of a chest of drawers as a change table. Measure up and get a piece of foam padding cut to fit and make some pillowcase-style covers for it.

Baby product holders
Those hanging shoe organisers are perfect for holding lotion bottles, washcloths, wipe containers, etc. Hang it over a drawer knob to keep everything handy.

Sheet sets
Pretty matching sheet sets are very sweet; however, they can be quite expensive. Instead use single-bed sheets, folded to fit and then fastened with elastic clips underneath. Make sure they are well tucked in. When baby gets into a normal bed you'll already have the sheets.

Baby Essentials

Cloth nappy cleaner
Using a bar of soap and a generic soaker will save you money and do just as good a job as the more expensive nappy soakers.

Generic brands
Generic nappy liners cut in half are great value for money. Urine-stained liners can be soaked in a generic antibacterial soaker and washed over and over again and used as dusters before they are thrown out.

Clothes line

Line-drying saves money and has the added advantage of bleaching and sanitising clothes in the sun.

Nappy rash treatments

Cornflour and bicarb soda make effective and cheap nappy rash treatments. A half cup of bicarb in the bath helps soothe sore bottoms and then a sprinkle of generic cornflour at each nappy change will keep little bottoms soft and smooth.

Baby wipes

Use face washers and water as baby wipes. Have a specific colour for them so you know that they are the baby-wipe washers. You can buy a pack of twelve washers from a discount store for around $6 and they will last and last. To go out, moisten a couple and put them in a zip-lock bag—they'll stay moist until you get home. Take a spare zip-lock bag in which to put any used ones.

Disposable nappy wipes

If you prefer disposable wipes, try this: cut generic nappy liners in half, place them in the bottom of a shallow, flat plastic container with a lid. Dilute baby bath wash with water and pour over the stacked nappy liners, cover to prevent them from drying out. Use these to wipe baby's bottom.

Disposable nappies

If you are using disposables, buy them in bulk on sale. Look for the 15 per cent- or 20 per cent-off sales and buy up then. If storage is a problem, lay-by them and collect them when you need them.

Nappy disposal system

Make your own nappy disposal system and save $70. Get a large bucket or bin with a tight-fitting lid (commercial ice-cream bucket), and some plastic grocery bags. Dab cotton balls with an essential oil such as lavender or lemon and drop into the bag. Add nappies and when the bin is full or at the end of the day, tie it up and put it in the rubbish bin.

Formula

Shop around for the best prices on your baby's formula. Prices vary so much, not just from brand to brand but from supermarket to pharmacy. Considering how much you will use, you can save a few hundred dollars on buying it at the right price.

uper Savings Hint: *We have a discount chemist near us. We chose the formula we wanted and compared the price with the local supermarket. We found we could save as much as $7 per tin by buying it at the discount chemist when it was on sale. We have saved over $200 already.*

Sterilising units

Rather than buying a sterilisation unit for $80, try boiling your bottles and teats in a saucepan for 5 minutes. Drain and store in a clean container with a lid to ensure they remain sterilised ready for use. Make sure you clean the bottles and teats thoroughly before setting them to boil.

I used a large saucepan and boiled everything (bottles, dummies, teats, caps, etc.) for 5 minutes on a rolling boil before transferring to a large plastic container with a lid to store until use. I did this twice a day until each baby was weaned.

School

Apart from Christmas, the start of a new school year is the most expensive time for parents throughout the country. With new uniforms, shoes, books, bags, pencils, lunchboxes and drink bottles to buy, saving money can be a real challenge. Don't get carried away by glossy pictures in the junk mail; most of what you have can be cleaned up and used again with just a little effort and some bright ideas.

Schoolbags and backpacks

Revamp last year's schoolbag or backpack by soaking it for a couple of hours in nappy soaker and then put through a gentle cycle in the washing machine. Give any stubborn marks a spray with stain remover and rinse or cover with a paste of bicarb soda and water. Leave overnight then scrub with a soft nailbrush. Dry thoroughly outside in the sun.

I've found the easiest way to do this is to prop up a broomstick and hang the bag upside down over it. This lets any water trapped inside drain out and the bag can dry completely. Choose a nice hot, sunny day to do this and the schoolbag should look almost new. If there are any repairs needed, try a cobbler before you throw it out. You can get zips and buckles replaced and straps re-stitched for just a few dollars, making what could have been rubbish perfectly usable once more.

Uniforms

Before buying new uniforms from the uniform shop, try the clothing pool or ask other mothers if they have old uniforms to pass on or sell. And don't go past the discount department stores. They sell good-quality, reasonably priced school clothes all year round. Keep an eye out for their back-to-school and 20 per cent-off sales and take advantage of lay-by if necessary.

Double strength

Boys can be very hard on the knees of their school trousers and they are expensive to replace on a regular basis. You can reinforce the knees by ironing onto the inside of each leg an iron-on patch of similar weight fabric. Then very carefully ditch stitch the edges of the patch onto the seams of the trouser leg. I have been doing this for years with my boys' pants and they are yet to go through the knees even though one of them is a keen sports player. Football, basketball and cricket haven't yet claimed the knees on their school trousers.

Removing hem marks

Back-to-school means letting down hems on dresses and trousers, which invariably leaves a dark line from the original hemline. To remove the mark left after letting down a hem, dampen a cloth with white vinegar, lay it on the crease and iron. The mark will disappear like magic.

No-sew hemlines

If you are time-poor or don't like hand-sewing, there is a product called hemming web that is designed especially for no-sew hemming. You buy it in a roll from any good haberdashers or specialty sewing store. It is so easy to use, just iron it between the fold of the hem and the garment using a damp cloth, and you have finished the hem! There are different weights for different fabrics, so ask for the one suitable for your garment.

Button savers

To save buttons on shirts (especially school shirts!) dab a little clear nail polish on the back of the button and across the centre front. This will help to stop the thread from coming undone and the buttons will stay on much, much longer. To replace buttons on school shirts, use dental floss to stitch the button back on, rather than conventional cotton. The dental floss is stronger and the button will stay on the shirt a lot longer.

School shoes

It always pays to buy quality shoes. They will outlast cheap fashion many times over and provide a stronger, more comfortable and healthier fit for your child. Rather than paying full price, try finding factory outlets, buy direct from manufacturers or buy when they are on sale.

Super Savings Hint: *School shoes are another big expense and here I believe that if you pay a little more in the beginning, you'll save in the long run. I have found in the past that the $15 and $20 shoes from discount stores just don't last as long as the $40–$50 shoes from shoe shops. I found that throughout the year I was buying at least two, sometimes three, pairs of cheaper shoes compared to just one pair of the more expensive shoes, especially for our boys.*

Schoolbooks

Covering books is every parent's back-to-school nightmare. It's a good idea to help protect your kids' schoolbooks from a year of abuse by making covers out of a durable material, such as brown paper. To cover books:

- Measure the height of the book, then measure the distance from the front to back covers. Add 15 cm to the two measurements (to create the inside flaps), and cut a piece of paper to this size.
- Open the book, and place it face down in the centre of the paper. To accommodate the spine, make two vertical cuts on the excess

paper at the top and bottom of the book, creating a flap. Fold the flap down and behind the spine, creating two notches. If this isn't possible, carefully trim the flap level with the bottom of the spine.

• Wrap the paper around the book, making sure the inside flaps are equal sizes. Fold top and bottom flaps over the side flaps and tape in place.

Decorating schoolbook covers

Print favourite photos of the children, stick these onto books and cover with clear contact for long-lasting book covers. Pictures of favourite sporting heroes, animals, etc. are also great to decorate book covers.

Lunchboxes and drink bottles

Watch out for sales to buy lunchboxes and drink bottles. You can get them cheaply if you buy them on sale in March/April. It is a good idea to buy them a year in advance and store them. Alternatively, don't buy new lunchboxes and drink bottles. Soak them overnight in a weak solution of bleach (2 drops of bleach to 1 cup of water; do check the bleach bottle as the strength of bleach can vary) to clean them up (they do get scruffy during the year) and then use bright stickers (from discount shops) to decorate them and name them. You can print out for free some really cute book/name labels from any number of clipart programs on the internet. Then use clear contact to stick them onto the lunchbox and drink bottle. The kids can also make their own stickers and labels from pictures they cut out of magazines. Glue them in place and cover them with clear contact to keep them in place.

Stationery

Stationery is cheap; look in catalogues. The major stationery retailers have great back-to-school sales in January and can be cheaper for most items than the discount shops. Look for specials on lever arch folders, bulk pens and pencils, rulers, sharpeners, paper refills, etc.

Super Savings Hint: *Last year I was able to get all my Year-7 son's stationery items for $11.48 from a major stationery store. I bought the specialty items, such as Textas, watercolour pencils, etc., from the discount department stores as they were cheaper there. It pays to shop around as I estimate that I saved over $100.*

Holidays

You can have a great holiday the Cheapskate way on any budget.

Planning Your Holiday

Local guides

Get the best deals on accommodation by using local resources. Look in local papers, check out the travel shows on TV and ask friends and family where they go and what they do. You'll get advice you can trust and find the very best deals available.

Motoring organisations

Motoring organisations, such as RACV, NRMA, RACQ, etc., have discounts available for members. They also have members' clubs and resorts, such as the RACV City Club in Melbourne CBD. Look for reciprocal arrangements with other organisations throughout the country.

Cheap airfares

Get the jump on cheap airfares by signing up for airline newsletters. They'll let you know ahead when they release special fares. Once you've booked your fares and finalised your holiday arrangements you can unsubscribe. Rejoin when you start to plan your next trip.

Use midweek rates

If you can't make a weekend break, an alternative is to go midweek. Often things such as car hire, accommodation and meals are cheaper—and you won't be battling the crowds.

Use the internet

There are many terrific last-minute deals available on the internet. They can be for local accommodation, airfares, holiday packages, car hire and tours. Use two or three websites to give you the best options. If you use them for domestic and international trips, they can save you 50 per cent off the normal price.

Off peak

If you are planning a holiday, consider going in the off-season or the shoulder periods if you do not have school-age children or if you are prepared to take your children out of school. You can potentially save hundreds of dollars on travel and accommodation and there will be far fewer tourists around.

Packages

Package holidays can be a great way to save hundreds of dollars on holiday plans. Packages can include fares, accommodation, meals, sightseeing tours and other activities. Research online for the best package deals available.

Packing

Reduce the amount of clothes and shoes that you take away. In most cases people don't wear or use everything they pack. Be aware that you'll be lifting heavy suitcases in and out of taxis and cars unnecessarily. Lay all your items on the bed and see what you can leave at home.

Fill the corners of suitcases and overnight bags with rolled clothes. This way you can distribute lots of items evenly throughout your case. This works best for casual clothes, such as jeans, jumpers and towels. Pack your shoes with socks to retain their shape. Pack all your toiletries and cosmetics in zip-lock bags. Flatten the bag and zip it closed. Changes in air pressure can cause leaks and this way the leak will be contained in the zip-lock bag.

Travel insurance

Take out travel insurance to cover hospital treatment or medical evacuation. Overseas medical costs are expensive and Medicare and Australian private health insurance will not cover you outside Australia. It may seem like an unnecessary expense, but if you have an emergency you will appreciate it. Make sure that your travel insurance is appropriate; if you are going on adventure activities, check the fine print. Not all policies will cover you for risky activities; even skiing may not be covered.

Accommodation

Budget accommodation

If you need accommodation, use the internet to research the best places to stay and the best rates. Investigate sites such as lastminute.com or check-in.com.au or wotif.com.au to see if there are any great deals on offer.

Camping and caravan parks

This is the most affordable holiday for your family. It takes time to set up so plan your holiday accordingly to minimise unpacking and repacking. Buy tents and equipment to make your trip enjoyable.

Look for sales or second-hand equipment or ex-demonstration tents and equipment.

Hiring a campervan can be a great way to travel. You can sightsee along the way, taking your time and enjoying your holiday. Campervans offer the perfect holiday travel solution—transport and accommodation all in one.

Caravanning is a great way to travel. Caravan parks offer power and laundry facilities and often have children's playgrounds and pools. You can buy a second-hand caravan, but shop around, there are heaps of options.

Overnight accommodation at caravan parks is inexpensive. They usually cost about half the price of a motel room and you have a small kitchen area if you need to cook dinner. They are not five-star; however, they are affordable, clean and often conveniently located. Many caravan parks now offer mobile homes as an accommodation option. They are like a mini house with bedrooms, bathroom, laundry and kitchen.

If you are going to use camping grounds often, look for discounts offered by the larger ones for your loyalty. You purchase a loyalty discount card making you eligible for considerable discounts in that park's chain for the year. There are two or three on offer so choose according to where you want to stay.

Farmstays

Farmstay holidays are the perfect alternative accommodation. They offer an unforgettable country holiday adventure and are fun for the whole family. A farmstay holiday provides an educational experience for city kids to join in and learn where eggs come from, how to milk a cow, feed baby animals and ride a horse. Accommodation varies from self-contained cabins to living in with the host family.

Bed-and-breakfast accommodation

An alternative to motels, bed and breakfasts (B & Bs) are ideal if you are en route, staying only a short time in each place. A comfortable place to sleep and a good breakfast to set you up for the day will add to your holiday enjoyment. Many B & Bs offer midweek and off-season discounts.

House swapping

Imagine having a real home away from home! Well, it is possible if you house-swap. It is as simple as walking out of your house in Australia and into a house in the country of your choice. House swapping is perfect for those who don't want to pay huge accommodation bills but still want comfortable digs. By house swapping, you save on accommodation, laundry costs and food by having a kitchen and laundry at your disposal. By the way, you can even arrange to swap cars.

HOUSE SWAP LINKS

House swap/home exchange
www.aussiehouseswap.com.au
www.ourhouseswap.com.au
www.peoplebrokers.com.au
www.homelink.org

House swap/home exchange
www.happyhousesitters.com.au
www.aussiehousesitters.com.au
www.housecarers.com
www.holidayhousesitters.com

Residential colleges

Many residential colleges lease rooms and apartments when the college is closed. For great budget accommodation in a central location close to tourist attractions, such as parks, gardens, museums, art galleries, zoos and more, you can't go past what they have to offer: clean rooms and hot showers. Public transport is usually excellent, another bonus if you are a visitor to the city.

Hostels

The Youth Hostels Association (YHA) is the best-known hostel program in Australia. It offers everything from dormitory sleeping for backpackers and budget travellers, through to twin, double and family rooms. Rooms are neat and spartan with communal bathrooms, kitchens and living areas. To access the program you need to join the YHA. The price is approximately $40 per person per year. This enables you to use YHA hostels in Australia and around the world. Some places will allow you to stay for free if you do a few hours of work for them. Check ahead for details of what their program is before you book your accommodation.

Cheap hotels

YMCA YMCAs are often used by younger people. They are an upmarket version of the YHA and focus on community and youth. YMCAs are often located in prime city locations and are generally clean and affordable. They offer twin, double and family rooms and usually have a cheap restaurant or café attached.

YWCA Similar to the YMCA though accommodation is generally only offered to women. They are very security conscious, so are a great option for women travelling alone.

Hotel chains There are many hotel chains that specialise in offering cheap accommodation. It is often better to use a hotel chain, as they will have to adhere to a star-rating system and a certain level of cleanliness. Do your research on the internet as there are sites where people will give you feedback about their stay.

Road Trips

Road trips can be a fun way to see the sights of the country.

Plan your route so you have time to stop at places of interest. Let the children research the things to see and do along the way and take a travel itinerary with you. They can use the internet to find the sites and your motoring organisation should have maps they can use to mark the way. Encourage them to keep a diary of the trip.

Pack a picnic for morning tea and lunch. Even if you've been away for a few days you can find a supermarket or deli to get fresh supplies. You'll be able to eat good food rather than a continual diet of junk.

Carry a bowl, mug and some cutlery for each member of the family. Buy and prepare your own breakfasts and save on motel/hotel meal fees. Look for all-you-can-eat restaurants and fill up at lunchtime (lunch can be half the price), then buy fruit for a snack for dinner. You'll save a fortune on meals.

Stop, revive, survive!

It is recommended that you stop for a break every two hours when driving on long trips. This is a great idea, not only to give you a break from driving, but also to give you the chance to have a drink and rehydrate and to stretch your arms, legs and back to stay limber. A fifteen-minute break will refresh you in mind and body, making the next leg of your journey safer.

Long trips with young children can be stressful—the confined space and length of time spent in the car can lead to squabbles. One way to stop bickering is to give each child a plastic coin bag (from your bank) filled with 10-cent coins. Every time there is 'he touched me' or a 'her leg's on my side' you collect 10 cents from the whiner. They get to keep the money left in the bag at the end of the trip. Try it and see how quiet and well behaved your little travellers can be.

Games to play

Have some fun games ready to keep the children busy so that they enjoy the travel part of their holiday.

- Keep track of how many different towns or cities you see on the road by putting a sticker on a map of Australia or writing them on a pad.
- See who can be the first to make a silly sentence using words that begin with letters found on numberplates, for example, WGL could be woolly goats laugh.
- Find the entire alphabet using the letters on numberplates of cars that you pass.

- Have each person pick a state and see who can spot the most numberplates from the state they've picked (exclude the state in which you are travelling).
- See who knows the capital of the state each time you see a numberplate representing a different state.
- Play 'I'm going on a trip and in my bag I'm going to pack' ... and then choose an object. The next person has to pack their bag with the first object and then add another object that begins with the same letter. As you go around to each person in the car the entire list has to be repeated in order with a new object added each time. When a person misses an object they are out of the game. The winner is the last person to remember the entire list.
- Make a rule that every statement has to be said in the form of a question. This is not as easy as it sounds but is a lot of fun. Someone might say, 'Did you see that car?' and the reply might be, 'Do you mean that yellow car?'. The response to that might be, 'Are you talking about lemon yellow or pale yellow?'. The next person could ask, 'Are you trying to confuse me?'. You would be surprised at how quickly a statement will come out of your mouth that cannot be turned into a question. Each person who fails to respond with a question is out of the game.

Car hire

There are companies throughout the world that specialise in providing cheap last-minute prices for vehicles that have not been booked. The cheapest prices come online one month from the hire date. Don't limit yourself to investigating one website; use two or three as they often have access to different vehicles and offer different prices.

We have used last-minute deals to hire cars and campervans. We checked over ten websites and found a huge variation in price, availability and service. If you want to use this process, do your homework. Likewise, you really have to be flexible and ready to travel when the car/van is available. If you have only two weeks and a fixed itinerary, it might be safer to book ahead; if not, enjoy the savings.

Buses

Bus passes
Within Australia and the United States bus passes can be a great way to get terrific value for money. You can get passes of various types through different bus lines where you can pay as little as $19 per day. You can't do that by car with hire and petrol costs!

Discount cards/student cards
Most local, regional and interstate buses will offer you a discount for student cards, seniors' cards or selected discount cards. Pensioners are open to discounts on most services, so take advantage of cheaper travel options.

Food

There is never good food at the places where buses stop for meal breaks. Greasy fried food that is mass-produced for fast feeding when the buses pull in makes meals most unappealing. Take some food along with you and use the breaks to walk around and stretch your legs.

Trains

Australia and the United States are not popular train-travel destinations. Europe, however, is fantastic. Eurail passes have been used by hundreds of thousands of tourists over the years and are a great way to travel around Europe. A Eurail pass is cost-effective and is much cheaper than hiring a car and paying for petrol and tolls on the highways. You can get passes for various time periods.

A Eurail pass is the best way to see Europe. We met stacks of locals and tourists with whom we could chat and share information. We practised the local language, took pictures of the countryside and had a marvellous holiday. There were always friendly B & Bs close to the stations and we often found the best cafes and restaurants with good cheap food close by. The intercity trains always ran on time and were clean and safe to use. We can highly recommend this way to travel.

Food

Train food is always expensive and is seldom tasty. Take a small thermal bag packed full of sandwiches, snacks and drinks for the trip. This helps to stave off motion sickness and makes your trip more enjoyable. Don't forget your camera; you can get some great shots.

Discount trips

Some train trips offer discounts for groups, seniors or pensioners. For example, using your local discount card might entitle you to some savings on train travel.

Cruises

Cruising is big business now with hundreds of holiday destinations to choose from. It is a great way to budget for a holiday as most of the costs are built into the price of the cruise. For example, accommodation, food, activities on board and some excursion trips onshore are included. Not included are alcohol, shopping and sightseeing trips.

Last-minute deals on the internet are available where cabins are offered at dramatically reduced prices. You may be able to get berths for 50 per cent of the normal price.

Planes

Some of the cheapest airfares around are only available on the internet. Use your computer to access and take advantage of these fares; you may save up to 60 per cent of the ticketed price. Just remember the additional fees and taxes for each fare. We have links to some of the best deals on
www.cheapskates.com.au/cheapskatesway

Minimise your cabin luggage. With security checks these days, the less you are carrying, the easier it will be for you to clear security. Everything will be X-rayed and thoroughly checked. See the Australian Government Travel website to find out about the latest instructions about cabin luggage: www.smartraveller.gov.au

Don't wear your contact lenses on long flights as they dry out, causing eye irritation and pain. You are better off to buy a pair of cheap prescription spectacles just for flying.

Be prepared and keep a small cabin bag packed with a change of clothes and a couple of days' supply of toiletries, basic stationery, important phone numbers and email addresses, a credit card and some coins. You can use it for emergency trips or take it on the plane if your luggage is misplaced.

Travelling in Comfort

Inflatable pillows are handy when travelling. Use them in cars, trains and planes. They are also handy once you've reached your destination if pillows are scarce. You can often get cheap travel pillows and other travel essentials at discount shops.

Avoid the pitfalls of travelling with credit cards. Instead, apply for a debit card and have each transaction taken directly from your bank account.

Don't pack toiletries if you travel a lot and stay in hotels/motels regularly. Use the complimentary packs provided in the bathrooms. You will need to pack only a toothbrush and toothpaste.

Read up on where you're going and check developments at your destination by reading country-specific travel advice available at www.dfat.gov.au/travel For some destinations these change frequently. Check that your travel insurance will cover you for delays or cancellations. For longer stays in any country or where the security situation is volatile, register your details with the Australian embassy or consulate. If in trouble, make your way to the consulate; they will either help you or contact your family for you.

Protect your personal information and make copies of your passport details, insurance policy, travellers' cheques and credit card numbers. Carry one copy and leave a copy with someone at home. It is wise to always carry extra copies of your passport photo with you, in your hand luggage as well as your suitcase or backpack.

Use email to keep in regular contact with friends and relatives back in Australia. Leave them a copy of your itinerary so they can follow your travels too. This is especially important if you are travelling alone or are moving constantly from place to place.

Take a travel nightlight with you, so that if you have to get up to the children at night or visit the bathroom, you are not stumbling around in the dark. You can buy them for around $2.95 from discount shops.

Utility Bills

There are many simple energy-saving tips that Cheapskates use to save a few dollars on their utility bills. Most are simple and with a bit of practice will become a habit. Encourage the children to get involved; after all, saving energy is about saving the environment as well as money.

Electricity and gas suppliers now offer flat payment plans. Your supplier reviews your total usage for the last twelve months and uses that total to work out a flat payment amount. You pay the same amount each fortnight or month throughout the year for your gas and electricity bills. While your bill will remain the same, it is in your interest to actively work to decrease your usage and save energy. This will ensure that if the costs rise throughout the year, you will not have an increased bill at the end of the year. Remember, if you have overpaid—they give you a refund or credit!

Gas

Turn the hot-water service down and save around $80 per year. Simply by turning the water temperature down, from hot to medium, you can potentially save up to $20 per quarter on your gas bill. You won't notice the drop in temperature and you'll be saving water too, as you'll use less cold water to cool the hot water down.

During the summer months make sure the pilot for your gas wall furnace or central heating furnace is turned off. Leaving the pilot burning during hot weather is not only a waste of gas but you will also be heating the house up too. You will be amazed at how much cooler your home will be with the pilot light turned off.

Turn the hot-water pilot off if you are going away for more than one night. It's pointless to be heating hot water when nobody is going to be using it. Modern hot-water services are quick to heat once they are turned on so hot water will only be a few minutes away once you get home.

Don't bother to pre-heat your oven for more than 5 minutes, especially if it's fan forced. Gas heat is instant heat, so unless you are cooking something delicate like a sponge cake or a souffle, pre-heating isn't necessary and a waste of gas and heat.

When cooking on a gas stove, use a steamer and cook in one pot, using one gas jet. Always be sure to use a flame that covers the base of the pot, not the sides! Turn it down if it is too high.

Electricity

Turn off appliances at the wall when you are not using them and cut your electricity costs. Having things such as televisions, VCRs, DVD players and computer monitors on standby uses electricity. Each TV uses approximately $26 per year; airconditioners use about $50 per year.

Turn off lights when you leave a room. It is cheaper to turn lights on and off than it is to leave them burning. Even turning a light off for a few minutes will save power and extend the life of your light bulbs.

Fluorescent lights use less electricity and provide up to three times the light of an incandescent light bulb. Consider swapping to compact fluorescent bulbs. They are cheaper to run and last up to eight times longer. There are new bulb-shaped ones that fit into all light fittings. Fluorescent lights are ideal for kitchens, family rooms and bathrooms and produce less wasted heat than a regular light bulb.

Dimmer switches reduce electricity usage and can lengthen the life of a light bulb.

Use lower-voltage lights on table lamps for reading or watching television.

Reduce overall lighting in non-work areas by removing one bulb in three in multiple light fittings. Consider using one large bulb instead of several smaller ones if bright light is needed.

Light settings should be on high when reading if using a three-way lamp to reduce eyestrain.

Lampshades should be white or light-coloured to get maximum light. Tall narrow lampshades or dark-coloured shades absorb light rather than reflect it.

Clean light bulbs as dust will cut the amount of light the bulb gives off.

Freezers should be kept full of food; it costs more money to cool dead air than food. Look for bulk buys or special offers and take advantage of them.

Ovens will heat more efficiently and use less electricity if there is more food in it. When possible, cook a few dishes at the same time. It may be a casserole for tomorrow night or something you can freeze for a quick meal after school sports. Remember, children love homemade cookies and cakes. While the oven is on, why not bake some biscuits?

Use energy-efficient devices such as pressure cookers, microwaves or electric frying pans and skillets. They cook your food faster and they use less energy than your stove or oven.

Heating

Keep your thermostat at between 18–20°C. If you are cold, put on a jumper or use a knee rug to keep the chill off while you're watching TV. Every 1°C increase in the thermostat setting increases heating costs by 15 per cent. Turn the heater off overnight. Put another blanket on your bed, get warmer pyjamas or make some wheat bags to keep your feet cosy and warm.

Stop warm air escaping from your home. Seal around windows, doors, heating ducts and power points with self-adhesive foam filler or insulation tape, which you can get by the roll from any hardware store.

Up to 30 per cent of heat loss occurs through glass. In winter, keep your curtains and blinds closed at night. By leaving them open, you're wasting over $2 for each square metre of glass per billing quarter! That's around $80 per quarter for the average home.

Living areas and bedrooms often don't need to be heated to the same temperature. If you are looking at installing central heating, investigate a zoned system. Keep doors to rooms you don't use closed and make sure the vent is closed too.

If you have a small area that you're only going to heat for a short time—for example, the kitchen in the mornings—then running a smaller, portable heater could be a more cost-efficient option than turning on the ducted heating or a fixed-space heater.

Cooling

Leave windows open at night to collect cool night air. In the morning, shut the drapes and block as much incoming sun as possible. You may feel like you live in a cave, but at least it's a cool cave. If you need some light, lounge on the lawn and leave the heat outside.

Plan summertime meals that don't use the oven; try eating more salads, cool fruity desserts, quick stovetop recipes and barbecue outdoors whenever possible to keep kitchen heat to a minimum. When you do bake, cook in batches. You can make 4 loaves of banana bread while your casserole is cooking and freeze the excess.

Turn off the airconditioner while you sleep. If your bedroom tends to get too warm, hang a damp sheet in front of a fan for a cool breeze.

Install ceiling fans. Moving air feels cooler and will make your room more comfortable. You'll find the fans to be a good investment in winter as well. Turning on a ceiling fan during winter will force down warm air that has risen to the ceiling.

Keep cool air inside by closing external doors and windows early in the morning, before the sun gets too high. Seal up any cracks around windows and doors to keep out hot air.

Check your insulation and if you don't have any, save up and buy some as soon as possible—it will significantly reduce your heating and cooling costs.

Use outside awnings and make sure they are down before the heat of the day and lift them after sunset, when the air is beginning to cool.

Don't block vents. Move your furniture away from air-conditioning vents and window units. Keep any shrubs outside trimmed so that they don't block vents.

Water

Make saving water a priority, not only to cut the cost of the water bill but also to preserve this precious resource. We live in the driest continent on earth and water conservation needs to become second nature to us all. These tips will save water, save you money, and ensure adequate water reserves for our future.

Conserve water by swimming in community pools or local lakes rather than splashing under sprinklers. For young children, host a pool party in the bathtub. Put a few inches of tepid water in the tub, dress the kids in their swimming suits and serve icy poles. Use beach towels to dry off.

Take shorter showers.

Switch to low-flow showerheads. There are different styles available so that you won't notice using less water and you'll be able to maintain your water pressure. Some units are available that allow you to cut off the flow without adjusting the water temperature knobs. By switching to water-saving showerheads, you may be eligible for government rebates.

Fix all drips and leaking taps in the house. Verify that your home is leak-free, because many homes have hidden water leaks. Read your water meter before and after a two-hour period when no water is being used. If the meter does not read exactly the same, there is a leak. Repair dripping taps by replacing washers. You can call a plumber or, if you are a handy person, talk to your local hardware shop and they will explain how to do it yourself. Fixing the drip will stop the annoying sound and save water (and money).

Showers use less hot water than baths, especially if you limit them to five minutes. If you are just going to wash your hair, do it over the basin.

Use the dishwasher for full loads and if you have a timer, set it to run during off-peak hours to save even more. Operate the washing machine only when it is fully loaded or properly set the water level for the size of load you are using.

Reuse water. Never put water down the drain when there may be another use for it, such as watering plants or cleaning. You can set up a simple grey-water recycling system to use the water from your washing machine. Check with your local council about requirements, restrictions and permits. Any grey-water treatment systems must be EPA-approved and storage systems installed by a licenced plumber.

Check for toilet leaks by adding food colouring to the cistern. If the toilet is leaking, colour will appear in the bowl within thirty minutes. Check the toilet for worn-out, corroded or bent parts. Most replacement parts are inexpensive, readily available and easily installed. Flush as soon as the test is done, since food colouring may stain.

Fix the toilet if the flush button sticks, letting water run constantly. If you can't do it, call a plumber or a local handyman to take a look as it will cost you a lot in wasted water.

Avoid flushing unnecessarily and dispose of tissues, insects and other waste in the rubbish rather than in the toilet.

Fill the bath with the minimum amount of water needed. Put the plug in before turning on the water; the initial burst of cold water can be warmed by adding hot water later.

Turn off the tap while shaving, washing your face or brushing your teeth. Brush your teeth first while waiting for water to get hot, then wash or shave after filling the basin.

When washing up by hand, fill one sink with soapy water, then half fill the other with hot water. A quick dip will rinse dishes of detergent residue.

Store drinking water in the refrigerator rather than letting the tap run every time you want a glass of cool water.

Defrost frozen food overnight in the refrigerator or by using the defrost setting on your microwave. Don't use running water to thaw meat or other frozen foods.

When adjusting water temperatures, instead of turning water flow up, try turning it down. If the water is too hot or cold, turn the offender down rather than increase the water flow to balance the temperatures.

Don't overwater your lawn. As a general rule, lawns only need watering every five to seven days in the summer and every ten to fourteen days in winter. A hearty rain eliminates the need for watering for as long as two weeks. Water lawns during the early morning hours when temperatures and wind speed are lowest. This reduces water loss from evaporation.

Don't water your street, driveway or footpath. Position sprinklers so that water lands on the lawn and shrubs—not on the paved areas. Consider using dripper heads rather than fine-jet sprays; you will find more water reaches the targeted area.

Install sprinklers that are the most water-efficient for each use. Micro and drip irrigation and soaker hoses are examples of water-efficient methods of irrigation and are easily installed.

Regularly check sprinkler systems and timing devices to be sure they are operating properly.

Raise the lawnmover blades to at least 7 centimetres. A lawn cut higher encourages grass roots to grow deeper, shades the root system and holds soil moisture better than a closely clipped lawn.

Avoid overfertilising your lawn as the application of fertilisers increases the need for water. Apply fertilisers which contain slow-release, water-insoluble forms of nitrogen.

Add mulch to your garden beds each year. A good thick layer of mulch will help to retain moisture in the soil, which saves you water. One good soaking is better than frequent sprinkles of water. Mulching also helps to control weeds that compete with plants for water.

Plant natives and/or drought-tolerant grasses, ground covers, shrubs and trees and group plants together based on similar water needs. Once established, they don't need to be watered as frequently and they usually survive a dry period without any watering.

Don't hose down your driveway or footpath. Use a broom to clean leaves and other debris from these areas. Using a hose to clean a driveway can waste thousands of litres of water.

Fit your hose with a shut-off nozzle that can be adjusted to a fine spray so that water flows only as needed. When finished, turn it off at the tap instead of at the nozzle to avoid leaks.

Don't leave sprinklers or hoses unattended. Garden hoses can pour out 1600 litres of water or more in only a few hours, so don't leave the sprinkler running all day. Use a kitchen timer to remind yourself to turn it off. And water early in the morning and late in the evening.

Use a commercial car wash that recycles water. There are many available now—both DIY and automatic—and all have to recycle water. If you wash your own car, park on the grass to ensure the water is soaked up by the grass.

Avoid installing ornamental water features (such as fountains) unless the water is recycled.

Water-saving Tips

- Create an awareness of the need for water conservation among your children. Avoid the purchase of recreational water toys that require a constant stream of water. If you use any water, make sure it is on the grass with a run-off to the garden.
- Be aware of and follow all water conservation and water shortage rules and restrictions that may be in effect in your area. There are water police issuing fines in some states now. Check with your state government or local council for the rules that apply to your area.
- Encourage your employer to promote water conservation in the workplace. Suggest that water conservation be put in the employee orientation manual and training program.
- Report all significant water losses (broken pipes, open hydrants, errant sprinklers, etc.) to the property owner, local authority or your water supplier as soon as possible. Every drop counts!
- Conserve water because it is the right thing to do. Don't waste water just because someone else is footing the bill; for example, when you are staying at a hotel. In many rural areas they are desperately short of water so give every Aussie a chance to have water and act responsibly.

- Try to do one thing each day that will result in a saving of water. Don't worry if the saving is minimal; every drop counts and every person can make a difference.
- If you're not sure whether indoor plants need watering, poke your index finger into the potting mix (about 2.5 centimetres should do it). If the mix is moist and clings to your finger, don't water. If it's dry and your finger comes out clean, water!

Phone

A Cheapskate is very conscious of how much money is spent on phone companies. Landline service fees are very high, local calls are still often at peak rates and mobile phones are extremely expensive to use.

Reduce telephone calls and monitor your calls and your children's by keeping a record beside the phone of every phone call you make. Teach the kids to log the call in the register every time they pick up the phone.

Set a phoning time to help reduce the amount of time the kids sit talking during an afternoon or evening. It is not so much to reduce the cost, but to give them time to undertake other tasks, such as homework and their chores around the house. Give them thirty minutes at 6 pm as their phone time.

Get to know the off-peak times to call regional areas, interstate or overseas. Keep any eye out for special deal times offered, usually at weekends.

If you like to speak to your interstate relatives regularly, ask them to call you one week and you can call them the next. Try to save your news for these times.

Put money into a jar every time you make a call. Even if you only put twenty cents in, it will make some contribution to the final bill.

Never forget to pay the phone bill—it can be a very costly exercise (approximately $50) to have the phone reconnected.

International phone cards can be up to twenty times cheaper than normal. Look for deals that include free local calls, free time for long-distance calls and other services such as the internet.

Investigate prepaid mobile phone plans for the kids. If their credit runs out you can still call them, giving you the reassurance that you can contact them if you need to, and the emergency number 000 will work if they get into trouble. This teaches them to budget their calls.

Cars

Your car is a major investment so it makes good sense to look after it. A well-maintained and cared-for car is a pleasure to drive and it will provide the best performance and fuel economy and the best resale value.

Car Care

Maintaining your car not only saves you money, time and energy, but it could also save lives. If there is a problem, fix it yourself or have it fixed by a quality car service centre as soon as possible—the longer you wait the more it is likely to cost, as other problems may arise.

DIY service is a simple thing you can do to save a lot of money. An average car service (not tune) can cost $80–$150. At the service they are checking all the fluid levels and filters in your car and changing your oil. You can do this yourself and save money. If you don't know how, consider doing a TAFE course to teach you the basics. It will cost about $100 and save you $250–$400 per year.

Regular servicing is essential to maintain your car and to ensure the safety of you and your passengers. Find a mechanic you trust. Ask around and check that they are qualified to do the necessary work. Remember, cheaper is not always the best value.

Check the oil levels. A car running with either too much or too little oil can damage the engine and cost a lot of money to fix. Top up the oil, if needed, and consider changing the oil and oil filter yourself if you are competent in this area. It can save you over $100 per year.

Check your tyres are correctly inflated. Tyres with incorrect air pressure will wear out sooner and give you poorer fuel economy. Check your manual for correct pressure (each car can vary) and next time you fill up check the pressure. Recheck monthly.

Replace worn tyres and save about 25 per cent by buying retread tyres or look at wrecking yards where you may pick up second-hand tyres with a good amount of tread for 50 per cent off new prices. Ensure they are balanced and fitted correctly. Keep the best tread tyres on the front wheels for better braking.

Check radiator water levels when your car is cool to avoid steam burns from a hot radiator cap. Newer cars will have a plastic bottle on the side that needs to be checked and filled. Check before long trips and in summer. Take a look at belts and hoses to ensure they are in good condition.

Check transmission and power steering fluid levels to ensure your car operates safely and efficiently. Older cars may not have these levels. If you have an automatic car or power steering, always check you have the right level of oil.

Check headlights, brake, parking and indicator lights are working and set to the right level. It is an offence to drive with any of your lights out of action.

Wiper blades should be checked at the start of winter. Often the heat on the windscreen in summer can damage the blades. It is fairly simple to change the blades or take the car to a service centre where they will do it. When the rain comes you want good wiper blades to clear the water from your screen.

Car paint can be preserved by washing the car with cold or lukewarm (never hot) water.

Run the airconditioner for at least ten minutes per month, regardless of the season. This procedure will maintain coolant pressure and avoid costly airconditioner breakdowns.

Battery maintenance requires corrosion to be cleaned off the battery terminals using a wire brush or steel wool. Clean the top surface with a mild solution of baking soda and water without letting it seep under cell caps.

Petrol

The dramatic jump in the cost of petrol has added roughly $14.00 a week to the cost of running our car. That's $728 in a year. Fuel prices are likely to rise even higher so here are some Cheapskate ways to save money on petrol and get maximum fuel efficiency and performance from your car.

Fill up first thing in the morning when it's still cool. This is especially relevant in summer as petrol is slightly denser when it's cool. As the petrol pumps measure volume you'll get better value for money buying early morning or late at night.

Service your car regularly. If you keep your vehicle well tuned you can reduce greenhouse gases by up to 5 per cent. Having your car well maintained will help it keep its resale value, too. Cars that run at peak efficiency have up to 20 per cent better fuel economy.

Know the price cycle of your local service stations. Find the days when the price is lowest and try to fill up then. It can vary by as much as 10 cents per litre, so be vigilant.

Save petrol dockets that you receive from supermarkets. These dockets offer up to 4 cents a litre off the bowser price for petrol and LPG, so they are worth using.

Buy from the distributor if you can. You could save up to 4 cents a litre. This is especially handy if you live in the country.

Maintain correct tyre pressure on your car. You'll find the information in your car's handbook. Under-inflated tyres reduce fuel efficiency by 2 per cent for every pound they are under-inflated and it also causes premature tyre wear, giving your tyres a shorter life. Over-inflated tyres can cause unnecessary wear. Use the recommended tyre pressure at all times.

Drive smoothly and avoid unnecessary acceleration. Keep a good distance from the car in front so you can anticipate and travel with the flow of traffic. This avoids unnecessary acceleration and frequent repetitive braking that wastes fuel—and it's safer.

Avoid using the airconditioner whenever possible. Air-conditioning reduces fuel economy by 10–20 per cent when operating. Use the air ventilation system instead. However, at speeds of over 80 kilometres per hour, using the airconditioner is better for fuel consumption than an open window.

Don't drive with open windows when travelling at high speeds. Open windows on the highway can reduce fuel efficiency by 10 per cent. It's much better to use the ventilation system or airconditioning.

Remove roof racks and other items that make your car less aerodynamic when they're not being used. Leaving them on only makes your car less fuel-efficient and costs you money.

Decrease idle times even on cold mornings. Cars don't need to idle for more than 30 seconds. Newer cars are designed to be driven almost immediately and letting your car idle for longer is a waste of petrol.

Switch off your engine when stuck in traffic jams or if waiting. You will save more fuel than is lost from the burst of fuel involved in restarting the engine and the increased wear and tear from doing this is negligible.

Remove excess weight from your car. Don't use your car as a storage space and add unneeded kilograms in weight. This unnecessary weight reduces the car's fuel efficiency by about 2 per cent for every 50 kilograms.

Reducing use is the easiest way to save petrol. Plan your trips so that you're doing a number of things in one go. You'll save time and fuel. If it's just a short trip, think about walking or cycling. If it's a longer trip, public transport or car-pooling may be alternatives.

Pets

We love our pets and to prove it these days we are spending more and more to keep them happy, healthy and well groomed. The pet industry in Australia is worth millions and is growing at between 15–20 per cent a year. We have pedigree and boutique cats and dogs that cost up to $1200 per animal. We keep exotic birds and tropical fish, mice, rats, reptiles, ferrets, horses and puppies with coats that match our handbags.

While feeding your pet is essential, food, clothes and veterinarian care are often well over budget and are areas where you can save a lot of money.

Cats

Forget expensive cat food. Cats like fish and meat. The fancy commercials on TV are to make us think their food tastes yummier. Don't pay for their expensive advertisements; your cat will be happy with leftover meat or fish and generic cat food.

Super Savings Hint: *Our cat likes to stay outdoors, only coming in for the evening and for food. Rather than paying $29.95 for a cat bed and $39.95 for a sheepskin pet cushion, the kids cut a hole in a sturdy cardboard box, painted the outside and we placed an old sheepskin rug that we bought from an op shop for $6 inside. The cat loves it and we saved $66.*

Cats like to snuggle into something warm. Old blankets, towels and fabric can make a great cat's bed. Try to leave it loose to allow the cat to scratch the fabric when stretching and playing and snuggle into it when sleeping.

Fur ball care—place a teaspoonful of petroleum jelly on your cat's front legs, squashing it into the fur so the cat has to lick it off and can't shake it off. If you look at the ingredients of the fur ball laxatives sold at the vet, the majority of the product is petroleum jelly with some flavouring.

 We use peanut butter as a remedy for our cat's fur balls. We have a small toy that we hide peanut butter in and he licks it for hours. It works like a treat.

Repel fleas by adding minced or powdered garlic to your cat's food. Fleas also hate mint! Gather up fresh mint from the garden and place some sprigs where your cat sleeps—this also works well as a repellent for mice and mozzies! Consider washing the bedding with a few drops of essential peppermint oil to help keep the cat flea-free.

Litter bags are overpriced. Use household bin liner bags, which cost half the price from a discount shop. Always put three or four on the tray, so you can quickly untie one, remove the content and you have the next one ready to go. Saves time and will stop the tray getting soiled.

Deodorised kitty litter works well, but is very expensive. Buy the cheapest kitty litter you can and mix in 500 grams of bicarb soda to make your own deodorised litter.

Treats and toys
Fabric and bells

Cats love to play with fabric they can push and claw and play. Sew a bell into each corner of a fabric square to make a toy that will keep them busy for hours.

Super Savings Hint: *The cheapest cat toy I have ever found was a felt square with a small bell firmly stitched to each corner that cost about 80 cents. Cats love the texture of the felt, they can dig in their claws, and the tinkling noise intrigues them as they move the felt around.*

Foil your cat

Cats love anything that rolls around, so keep your moggy amused with a ball of aluminium foil! Tear off a length of foil and scrunch it up into a tight ball.

Milk bottle caps

String three lids from milk bottles together, carefully knotting the ends to prevent the lids coming off and throw it down in front of your cat.

Scratching mats

If your cat prefers the furniture to his scratching post, try placing carpet samples around the house. This gives the cat a variety of surfaces to scratch rather than using the furniture. You can buy them from market stalls or you could ask a carpet retailer for some scraps from a discontinued range.

> **Outside a house one day, I saw a carpet layer carrying out some old carpet to throw out. I stopped and asked the fellow for some squares for my cat. He picked out some clean pieces, cut it into small squares and I have enough mats to keep my cat happy for years.**

Dogs

Luxury dog food costs about $3 per can, doggie coats about $45 and flea tablets $120. As a Cheapskate, you can have these for your pet, but at reasonable prices.

Buy generic brand dog food and you can save a lot of money. A tin of a popular brand of dog food costs $2.82 whereas you can get a generic brand for $1.29. Depending on how much your dog eats this could equate to over $300 per year. Don't be fooled into thinking that paying more means better food; it often means you are paying for the TV advertising.

You can save money on food and expensive vet bills simply by cutting back on the amount of food your dog eats. In many cases dogs are fed far more than they need. Add leftover meat, vegetables or bread to your dog's food, mix it up and your dog will love it. This adds variety to their meals and prevents waste in your kitchen.

Dog Food

1 tablespoon olive oil

500g cheap minced meat

2 cups cooked rice or pasta

1 carrot, finely chopped

1 potato, finely chopped

½ teaspoon finely chopped garlic

2 teaspoons finely chopped parsley

½ teaspoon basil

Heat olive oil in a saucepan over medium heat, add meat and fry until browned. Set aside. Return pan to heat, add rice or pasta, vegetables, garlic, parsley and basil and cook until vegetables and rice are tender. Combine with meat and store in airtight containers. This will last for about two weeks and freezes well.

Cook your dog food on the barbeque using a large steel pot that you can pick up quite cheaply from discount stores or during sales at retail stores. This keeps the smell of the cooking dog food out of the house. Add detergent and hose down the pot after use and store in the garage or garden shed.

Super Savings Hint: *We make our own dog food and save over $5 a week ($250 per year). The dogs like it better than tinned food as we use good-quality meat bought at a discount butcher. As a bonus, I have noticed the dogs have trimmed down a little.*

Bedding

Sew a second-hand inner tube into an old grain sack and inflate. The inner tube makes a comfy ring for the dog to lie on. The inner section breathes and is kept off the ground to keep the bed dry. A large dog bed is $40: this one will cost you 20 minutes of time. You can get a grain or seed sack/hessian bag from a feed supplier and an inner tube from a tyre repairer.

To control fleas and mange, add a teaspoon of vinegar to your dog's drinking water, put garlic in your dog's food and grow mint in pots close to where your dog sleeps.

Flea shampoo for dogs—mix one part Dettol, two parts dishwashing liquid and three parts water and store in a bottle for future use. Use enough to get a good lather on your dog's coat.

To prevent flea re-infestation, wash the dog's bedding in hot water with oil of pennyroyal added to the wash. This oil can also be added to water in a spray bottle and sprayed on cushions, lounges, doorways, etc. **Pennyroyal should never be used around pregnant women or pregnant animals.**

Treats and toys

For small dogs, you can use your children's old windcheaters or buy one from an op shop to make dog jackets. Cut the sleeves off the windcheater and, using the wristband for the neckband, cut out holes for the front legs.

For larger dogs, chop the legs of adult-sized track pants and cut holes in one of them for the dogs legs. If you find it is too wide simply make a hem and thread a length of elastic through.

Look at discount stores for a large range of useful toys for your dog. The toys are often the same as those sold at the vet or pet shop, they are just a lot cheaper.

 I have a red heeler who loves to play with used plastic milk containers. While a puppy we used to give her the containers and she would chew at the lid until she got it off. We would leave a little milk in the container for her as a reward.

Fish

Bulk buy fish blocks from your pet shop or pet supply wholesaler. You can save 30 per cent on the price of buying smaller packets. Buy enough for one year and store in an airtight container.

Buy fish flakes by the kilogram rather than in small containers. You will save up to 40 per cent on the cost. Store the food in a large, resealable container. If your children feed the fish, put some into a smaller container to prevent overfeeding and accidents.

Substitute fish-flavoured dry cat food for fish flakes and save a fortune. A box of dry cat food should last you at least 6 months, depending on the number of fish you are feeding.

Grow your own weed and save at least $50 a year. You'll need a bucket, a sunny spot, some water and a sprig of weed. Place the weed and the water in the bucket and sit it in the warm, sunny spot. It will grow—well, like a weed—and you will have a constant supply to restock your fish tank.

For healthier goldfish, occasionally add 1 teaspoon of non-iodised salt to 2 litres of fresh water at room temperature and put your goldfish in it for about 15 minutes, then return them to their tank.

To clean the fish bowl, rub the inside of the fish tank with plain, not iodised, salt to remove hard water deposits, then rinse well before returning the fish to the tank.

Birds

Smother a pinecone bird feeder in peanut butter, roll it in bird seed that is appropriate for native birds and hang it in a tree. The birds will love it and you can renew the seed over and over.

Use macramé pot holders as bird feeders. Place a shallow terracotta dish in the pot holder, fill with seed and hang in a tree. You'll find macramé pot holders in op shops and at trash and treasure markets.

Treats and toys

Cuttlebone from cuttlefish, can be picked up on the beach and birds just love it! Wash it well and dry thoroughly before giving it to your bird. This is an excellent source of calcium for your bird, too.

When on holiday as children we used to walk along the beach and collect cuttlefish for our pet bird. Over the course of our two- or three-week holiday, we would collect enough for the whole year. It was fun and great exercise as we walked and ran along the beach for miles.

Birds love to play with toys. To ensure you keep your bird busy, rotate toys in the cage. Bells, knotted rope, mirrors and small balls make excellent bird playthings. Rotating toys saves money on having to buy new toys all the time.

Christmas

Christmas can be a huge financial drain with its parties, presents, food and decorations. Many people get caught up in the fun and place themselves in enormous debt—especially credit card debt—at this time of year. There are many ways for you to have a fabulous family Christmas without all the debt. Enjoy the season and be a Cheapskate: you may save $1000–$3000 by doing so.

Presents

Being a Cheapskate allows you to give better gifts for less money. Rather than joining the Christmas crush, Cheapskates learn to do their shopping earlier in the year. By doing this, they save money, buy in a relaxed environment where they can get exactly what they want and time it to coincide with great sales offers.

Use discount vouchers There are many coupons, discount vouchers and sale offers that arrive in the letterbox or that are printed on checkout chits and are given out as a thank you gift with purchases. Use these wisely throughout the year to get the best savings on your Christmas presents for family and friends.

Use credit-card reward points Most credit cards earn reward points. Rather than waiting to use them on airline flights—which seem impossible to get unless you book two years in advance—use your points to buy the goods they offer in the rewards program. They sometimes have special deals and you can get some great products.

Buy direct from manufacturers, importers and wholesalers Many manufacturers, importers and wholesalers sell direct to the public, so you can get some terrific deals—often buying for 20–50 per cent below retail prices. Keep your eyes open in industrial and commercial areas for direct-to-public signs.

Buy at discount stores Discount shops often get a great deal on super cheap stock from manufacturers and importers. You can find tasteful quality items that may be as heavily discounted as 50–70 per cent below retail prices. Do your homework to ensure you get good-quality products.

Buy online and save While I am not a fan of eBay as I have watched far too many items sell above market price, I do find bargain prices at some online shops. Again, you must do your homework as there are sharks out there. Try to find medium-sized companies selling at genuine sale prices.

Buy presents on sale. Shopping at Christmas can be a misery: fighting to get a car park, impossible crowds in the stores, ridiculous queues at checkouts and overpriced goods for sale. Begin your Christmas shopping on Boxing Day. Make a Christmas list for next year and take advantage of the sales to get your Christmas presents. There is no need to ever pay full price for anything.

Lay-by presents on sale, you won't be charged interest and they store the goods until you are ready to pay them off. This is a great way to buy and hide the children's presents.

Buy amusement park tickets for the family to use on holiday. Consider buying a family pass for the whole family if you have the money.

Purchase family memberships to the zoo or museum.

Have an emergency gift bag Sometimes you get invited to parties at the last minute or children have to give a new friend a gift.

Rather than paying full price, buy gifts to be used for such emergencies in the sales.

Plants While it is easy to pick up the phone and send a bunch of flowers, why not select an unusual plant from the nursery to show you care.

Buy a subscription to the *Cheapskates Journal* It costs only 10 cents per day or $36.50 per year and it can help your friend of family member get out of debt and be able to afford a great lifestyle.

Cellar door wines Look out for special deals to buy your Christmas wine in bulk. You can buy a case of last season's wine direct from a cellar door for much less than shop prices. Buying direct from the wine maker gives you a chance to share the story of the wine as well.

Book clubs Many book clubs have fantastic books for all ages at discounted prices. You will be able to do all your Christmas shopping quickly and easily from the catalogue and have it delivered to your door.

Use free samples Many companies offer free samples of their products. Send away and collect these over the year, then at Christmas add these to gift baskets that you make up.

For children

Coloured pens Children love gel pens and the huge range of colours they come in. Add a sketchbook, pencil case and some shapes to copy and you have a great gift.

Puzzles Look around in the sales for puzzles. If you choose a jigsaw puzzle, think of including a neat plastic container in which to store the pieces.

Marbles Remember the fun you had as a child playing marbles? Be sure to add some wool for the circle and some simple rules on a card that they can read. Be prepared to play a game or two with them until they get the idea of how to play. This is not suitable for smaller children.

Pickup sticks Yes, another oldie and a goodie. You can buy commercial packets or make your own by cutting the sharp ends from skewers or using craft sticks to make a set. Be prepared to teach the children how to play and perhaps give them a card with the rules.

Novelty clothes Gifts of novelty clothing, such as socks, headbands and underwear, can be fun. Find clothes that are funny or represent sports teams they follow. The best time to buy these is at the end of a season, for example, the footy stuff is dirt cheap following grand final day.

Hair Accessories Girls love to make themselves look special. Buy a collection of pretty hair accessories from a discount store or go to a wholesaler or importer.

Music For young children it is easy to buy popular children's songs. Give a voucher for teens as their tastes change and often they like MP3 or digital formats. Watch for sales or buy online from discount vendors.

Posters Children love posters of their favourite stars. For young children try Bob the Builder, Fairies, Wiggles, etc. With the older children, it may be best to check with the teen or parent what they currently like in music.

Movie tickets If you are going to give movie tickets to a few people, consider buying the bulk ten-ticket books. You will save

$1–$3 dollars per ticket. If you are posting tickets interstate, ensure the cinema chain you choose operates in that area.

Cashed-up balloons This is fun when the children are older. Insert cash—coins and notes—into balloons, blow up the balloons, tie them in a bunch and give them to the kids. Please **do not** give this to smaller children, as burst balloons can be dangerous.

Homemade gifts

An increasingly common gift-giving trend is to give with heart. This may be a hamper you have carefully put together that you know the recipient will love or it may be making a present from scratch. Following is a list of inspiring ideas.

Make personalised calendars from your children's art work for grandparents. Buy twelve large sheets of paper, punch a hanging hole in the top and stick on the pictures and calendar details (printed out from the computer).

Works of art Frame a yellowing piece of sheet music in an old battered frame with character or distress a new frame by roughing up the finish with sandpaper. Glue a swag of dried flowers to the bottom of the frame and attach a wire-trimmed bow to the top to finish off.

Beeswax candles Buy sheets of beeswax and a length of wick from a craft or variety store. Heat the beeswax lightly with a hairdryer and place the wick, cut about 2 centimetres longer than the sheet, near the edge of the beeswax. Roll up the beeswax to form candles. Trim wick, if necessary. If beeswax starts to crack, warm again with the hairdryer.

Shoebox road maps Cover a shoebox with old road maps and fill it with current road maps to give to a traveller. This is a wonderful idea if you have a friend who is going on a road holiday around Australia or going overseas and travelling by car.

Craft baskets If you are a crafty person and have an assortment of fabric and bits and bobs, why not make up some baskets for your friends complete with instructions and everything they need to make a wonderful craft memento, such as:

Cross-stitch—pattern, threads and cloth

Mini quilt kit—fabric squares, thread and instructions

Scrapbooking kit—paper, stencils, layout guides and gel pens

Scarf—knitting needles, yarn and a pattern

Beading—beads, wire or thread, needle, clasps, small pliers

Gift hampers It doesn't take long and can be very economical to make your own hampers for Christmas. If you buy six or more bottles of wine from some retailers you get 20 per cent off.

Baked gifts Bake a batch of cookies and decorate with red and green glace cherries or make some chocolates or small Christmas puddings. Wrap in a red or green napkin and tie with lots and lots of curling ribbon.

Share favourite recipes Write out a favourite recipe, include two or three of the ingredients, a mixing bowl, spatula, baking tray, etc. and place in a wicker basket. Decorate with ribbon and a homemade card.

Winter warmer soups Write out some of your favourite soup recipes on a decorative card, add different kinds of soup mix and dried beans in zip-lock bags and place in a bowl or box.

First-aid kits Make up a first-aid kit with Band-Aids, antiseptic cream, tweezers, small scissors, etc. and place in a zip-lock bag for easy storage in a glove box or bathroom cupboard.

Bathroom baskets Fill a basket with soap, shower cap, bubble bath, bath oil and a face washer. Place on bright or decorative paper and then wrap the basket in clear or coloured cellophane and add some ribbon.

Bookworm baskets Start collecting books—novels, cookbooks, hobby or craft books. Look for sales and special price offers. Add these to a larger basket or box with a card and give it to a friend who loves to read.

Kitchen baskets Fill a basket with spatulas, measuring cups, oven mitts, tea towels and an apron. This is particularly useful for a young couple or someone moving into their first flat.

Garden baskets Gardeners will appreciate a wire basket or bucket filled with packets of seeds, gardening tools, gloves, water saturates, fertilisers or garden decorators, etc.

Car care buckets Fill a plastic bucket with car care products for a car enthusiast. Keep an eye on special discounts from car or retail stores for polishes, washes and deodorisers.

Children's toy boxes Fill a crate with puzzles, books or toys that you have bought at sales throughout the year. As a variation, fill a smaller toy box/plastic container with games, toys or books that are suitable to take in the car, plane or train for the next holiday.

Picnic baskets Fill a basket with a picnic set of cups, plates, tablecloth, napkins and some plastic containers. Make a two-piece setting for a young or newly wed couple or for the grandparents.

Nut treats Buy some pretty glass dishes that are on special throughout the year and buy a variety of fresh nuts. Package them with decorations in a basket. These are practical and useful especially for a couple who entertains a lot. Avoid giving this to families with young children or allergies to nuts.

Fresh fruit and vegetables If you have a garden patch then why not share some of your fruit and vegetables. Alternatively, visit a grower and buy some exotic fruits or vegetables.

Banana cakes Bake a banana cake and include the recipe and ingredients. Alternatively make banana bread, include some good coffee and a card with suggestions for a wonderful Sunday brunch.

Natural and tasty baskets Fill a basket with packets of raisins, rolled oats, granola, chopped almonds, dried apricots, coconut, etc. You might add some glass jars for storage or small lunch-sized plastic containers so they can be carried to work for a lunch or mid-morning treat.

Stationery sets Include scissors, pens, pencils, rulers, paper clips, glue sticks, memo pads, etc. and place your goodies in a neatly decorated box. This is a great gift as we all use stationery and giving it in a box means that it can be safely stored in its container.

Painter's baskets Fill a basket with a paint set, a variety of brushes and pencils, a sketchpad or canvas and a how to paint book. This makes a wonderful gift for someone who has retired or is taking time off work.

Gourmet coffees These delicious flavoured-coffee mixes are a cheap and easy Christmas gift. Store them in attractive glass jars with tight lids and you have a gift that any coffee lover would appreciate. These mixes can be made ahead ready to give at Christmas. Hunt around for a mug or cup and saucer to complete the gift. Make a label with the instructions for making up the coffees and tie it around the neck of the jar.

Cappuccino Mix

½ cup good-quality instant coffee

½–¾ cup castor sugar

   (depends on strength of coffee)

1 cup instant non-fat powdered milk

1 teaspoon ground cinnamon

Combine ingredients in a food processor or blender and blitz well.
Wait for dust to settle and transfer to an airtight container.
Use 2 tablespoons per cup of hot water.

Cafe Au Lait Mix

½ cup good-quality instant coffee

½ cup castor sugar

2 cups instant non-fat powdered milk

½ teaspoon ground cinnamon

Combine ingredients in a food processor or blender and blitz well.
Wait for dust to settle and store in an airtight container.
Use ¼ cup for each ⅔ cup of hot water.

Swiss Mocha

½ cup good-quality instant coffee

½ cup castor sugar

1 cup instant non-fat powdered milk

2 tablespoons cocoa powder

Combine ingredients in a food processor or blender and blitz well.
Wait for dust to settle and store in an airtight container. Use
1 tablespoon for each ¾ cup of hot water.

Presents for children to make

Make gifts for family and friends and get the kids involved in the
spirit of things. Make some time in the weeks leading up to
Christmas to be creative with the children. They can make gifts for
grandparents, teachers, classmates and neighbourhood or sporting
club friends. Don't forget to give them some ideas and maybe a little
help to make Mum and Dad something too.

Read a story onto a CD. This is a great idea for grandparents who
live interstate or overseas.

Frame photos of happy events to remember the good times
shared. Children love photos—especially if they are in the picture.

Encourage the kids to make Christmas ornaments and to be
creative in what they make and how they decorate them.

Gift baskets can be fun for the children to put together. They can
fill them with precious pictures, photos and crafty items they have
made throughout the year. You can pick up baskets in discount
shops or reuse ones that you may already have.

Decorative gift boxes Use a shoebox or some other sturdy box, cover with wrapping paper, wallpaper, fabric or contact and get the children to cut out or draw pictures and glue these to the outside of the box. For variety try adding cut-out pieces of fabric or shapes, beads or sparkles. Apply a clear lacquer over the top and add ribbon. These make great gift boxes, especially for large or oddly shaped gifts.

Papier-mâché pots To make papier-mâché, cut up old egg cartons or newspaper and mix with water. Use an empty pot plant for the mould and cover with a thick coat of papier-mâché. When the papier-mâché is dry, turn it out of the mould and paint it or tie a length of ribbon around the top. Add a packet of flower seeds if you like.

Decorative bath-time treats Save two or three empty food jars (baby-food jars are good), decorate with pretty decals, stickers, ribbons and sparkles and fill them with bubble bath, bath salts or relaxation crystals that you have bought from a discount shop. Fill the tops of the jars with cotton balls (absorb any moisture) and cover the jar tops with fabric.

Painted jam pots Take a visit to a local berry or fruit orchard, pick some fruit and make some homemade jam with the children. Place the jam in a decorated jar and tie a ribbon around it. Make sure you make enough for the children to save and eat throughout the year. For variety, visit a honey grower and get some local honey.

Card, Decoration and Gift-wrapping Ideas

Buy cheap cards and personalise them by adding a nice thought, favourite quote or special message.

Design cards on the computer. You can write your message, add a photo or colour in pictures and then print. Have some textured paper on hand to make the card look interesting and fun.

Get the kids involved; you will be encouraging their creativity and their recycling skills. I save old cards, magazines and calendars—you can find some beauties at opportunity shops for under 50 cents—and cut out pictures that might be of use. I also keep bits of coloured card, paper, ribbon and thread. Any tiny pictures can be used for gift tags. Brown paper makes great wrapping paper and looks very effective if it is tied up with coloured raffia or string. I have worked out that I save around $200 a year by doing this.

Santa sacks Make sacks from Christmas fabric and ribbon and personalise them with the children's names. Santa puts his presents in the sack and ties it shut. These can be reused every year, saving money and time and creating a lasting memory.

To make card hangers, spray red paint onto a packet of wooden clothes pegs, glue a wooden angel onto the middle of each peg and clip the pegs onto a length of gold cord. Tie a big knot in each end to stop it unravelling. Attach the cord to the mantelpiece and add your Christmas cards. Total cost $5.95 for a fifty-card hanger—a saving of $20.65 on buying fifty ready-made card pegs from Christmas shops.

Lolly topiary trees Large topiary trees are sold in department stores for $24.95 each. You can make one for less than $10. Buy a terracotta pot (for around $1), hunt around the backyard/park for a strong, rustic-looking twig to use as the stem. Stick the stem into florist foam or oasis using a quick-set glue. Once dry, spray the pot and stem gold. Stick a large foam ball ($2 from the market) onto the top of the stem, then attach wrapped lollies (Columbines or something similar) onto the ball with a little blob of Blu-Tac until it is completely covered.

Decorated glass baubles are quick and easy to make. Buy boxes of twelve baubles in all colours from discount shops. Depending on the size, they range in price from $2–$6.95 for twelve. Decorate with stickers and decals rather than paints. Buy sheets of gold, silver and rainbow-coloured stickers for $2.95 a sheet. Each sheet makes at least twelve baubles, if not more. If you choose a coloured ball, all you need to do is stick on your Merry Christmas decal. If you want to add the year, use glitter glue in a coordinating colour under the Merry Christmas. You can make these baubles for around 65 cents each!

Pasta Christmas ornaments can be made out of different-shaped pasta that has been spray-painted gold or silver and tied with gold or silver thread.

Popcorn balls are easy and inexpensive to make. Cook popcorn without adding salt or butter, cool and then thread with a needle onto fishing line or similar-strength thread. Roll up into balls or leave as long threads to drape on the Christmas tree. As a variation, place threaded popcorn onto a sheet of plastic, spray with adhesive and sprinkle over glitter.

Candy canes are cheap, yummy to crunch on and are readily available from about October through to December. They are great for holiday decorating in our climate because they don't melt!

- Hang candy canes on the Christmas tree. They look pretty and if visitors have children, they can pick a cane off the tree as a special treat
- Attach candy canes to tinsel using Blu-Tack and string a row across the tops of doorways, mantelpieces and windows. You can use these year after year
- Use candy canes to decorate wreaths
- Make Christmas cards using candy canes by joining two canes together to form a heart shape and attaching them to the front of the card. Write a special message inside each one
- The children can give Christmas cards to their friends and classmates and stick a candy cane onto the envelope as an edible decoration and small gift
- Make candleholders for table centrepieces. Buy 1.5-centimetre-diameter wooden dowelling and cut into 10-centimetre sections. Spray-paint each section red and use hot glue to attach the candy canes to the dowel (upside down with the hook away from the dowel). The bottom of the candle rests on the dowel in the centre of the candy canes. Add some greenery to the bottom or tie a ribbon around the centre
- Put a couple of candy canes in gift baskets or use them with a ribbon as decoration on top of Christmas gifts

- Break up candy canes, drop them into a 2-litre bottle of dry ginger ale and add to your Christmas punch
- If you're having a sit-down Christmas party, use candy canes for each place setting
- Chop up candy canes and sprinkle them on ice-cream
- Use crushed candy canes to decorate your cut-out Christmas cookies
- Try making decorative ornaments with candy canes. Reindeer are easy. Glue two small woggly eyes onto the side of the hook part, and then twist a pipe-cleaner around the top of the hook as antlers. This is simple enough for the kids to do and they look great hanging from the Christmas tree
- Tie candy canes in bundles of five with ribbon and stack them in a pretty dish to decorate tables
- Make a candy cane vase by gluing candy canes, curved side up, around an empty peanut butter jar. Fill with red flowers for a unique Christmas table decoration

Handmade wrapping paper Make beautiful wrapping paper out of waxed paper and flowers and leaves picked from the garden. Place a towel on a table, roll out as much waxed paper as possible, waxed side up, and sprinkle over petals, leaves and small flowers or different shaped leaves or small cute cut-outs. Place a sheet of waxed paper, waxed side down, on top and press with a warm iron. You can make a fresh batch any time you need wrapping paper and it will always be different. Save some of the children's Christmas and birthday cards and wrapping paper and cut out characters ready for your next batch.

The Wrapping Box—*You have ten minutes before you leave for the party, and you haven't wrapped the gift, or written on the card. In fact, you don't even have a card. What do you do? Panic? Stop on the way to buy wrapping paper and a card? Why not be prepared and start a wrapping box? It's a simple thing really. I have a plain old brown cardboard box that fits on the top shelf in the cupboard.*

My wrapping box includes: wrapping paper (six sheets for $1), cards for all occasions (50 cents each from a discount shop), sticky tape, stickers, ribbons, bunches of silk and dried flowers to decorate gifts, plain scissors and two pairs of fancy scissors to make decorative edges around cards and gift tags, rubber stamps, stamp pads, Textas, gel pens, glue sticks, liquid glue, tubes of glitter glue and bottles of glitter.

I top the box up at the post-Christmas sales with Christmas paper, etc. and throughout the year as I see things on special.

Christmas decorating

It's easy to change the look of a room with a few simple, easy-to-make, inexpensive decorations. You first need to decide on a colour scheme. The traditional red, green and white is always popular, but what about the colours of summer: vibrant blue, sunny yellow and lime green? The colours of the bush are pleasant and soothing to the eye and are easy to replicate. Gum tree greys and bottlebrush red bring a hint of the outdoors indoors.

Even though it can be unbearably hot on Christmas Day, there is nothing quite as spectacular as lit candles on the dining table. Candle arrangements don't have to be expensive or complicated. To help your candles burn longer, keep them in the fridge until you are ready to light them.

Candle wreath Use a 15-centimetre cane wreath. Place a red pillar candle in the centre of the wreath. Take a poinsettia pick (the stem of an artificial flower), gently pull the flowers off the stem and evenly hot-glue them around the wreath. Fill the gaps with the poinsettia leaves. Spray lightly with gold paint to highlight.

Candle grouping Group together three church candles of different heights, tie a length of gold ribbon around the centre and cover the knot with a gold bow. Stand the candles on a glass cake plate and sprinkle wishing stones (flat, coloured glass pebbles found in craft shops) around the base of the candles.

Tea lights Use small glass jars, such as old Vegemite jars, to make Christmas tea lights. You can buy sheets of Christmas decals from discount shops for $1.50–$2. Decorate the jars with the decals and place a tea light inside. When the candle is lit, the decals will reflect the light and the jars will look like they are made of stained glass. Tea lights can be bought very cheaply—a pack of 100 for around $3.95!

Paper chains Red and green paper chains strung from corner to corner add a festive Christmas air to any room. These are easy to make with strips of coloured paper and a bottle of paste. The children can make them in an afternoon, and they can be attached to the cornice with a dob of Blu-Tack.

Window trims Trim the windows with swags of tinsel. Use two colours twisted together for a plush, vibrant look. Pin each end to the top of the window frame, leaving a tail hanging down about halfway. Drape the tinsel across the top of the window, pinning it in the middle to create a swag. Place a decoration in the middle to finish it off. Tinsel is available in a great range of colours and is inexpensive. Try a discount store as they often have great bargains in the decoration department.

I made calico angels that are used as part of the window trim every year. They look great with the coloured tinsel.

Table centrepiece Glue tea light candles into a star or heart shape. Turn them over and give the base and sides a spray of gold or silver craft paint, let them dry and then tie a narrow ribbon around the outside edge. The star shape can be sprayed gold, allowed to dry and sprayed with a thin coat of adhesive. Turn it upside down and then shake some silver or gold glitter over it. Carefully turn on its side and sprinkle glitter around the edges. Allow to dry before you use it. These make great decorative centrepieces, or are fabulous for lighting dark corners of your living room.

Placemats and coasters This is an innovative way to recycle old Christmas cards and you can have a new set every year. To make coasters, let the kids cut up old Christmas cards and glue the pictures to circles or squares of coloured paper the size of a drinks coaster or placemat. Laminate by placing them between two layers of clear or coloured contact paper. To make placemats, have the kids make a collage of pictures on a piece of coloured A4 paper. When they have the arrangement in place, glue it to the coloured paper. Laminate between two layers of clear contact.

Lolly wreath Bend a wire coathanger into a circle. Take a length of green tinsel, tape one end to the top of the circle and tightly twist the tinsel around the wire, taping it at the end. Use small blobs of Blu-Tack to stick wrapped lollies around the wreath.

 I use green-and-white wrapped lollies with green tinsel. If you use purple or pink tinsel, Columbine caramels in their purple, pink and blue wrappers look fabulous.

The scents of Christmas Make small bowls of potpourri by combining cinnamon sticks, whole cloves, allspice, citrus peel and pine cones and place them around the house.

Shine Spray pine cones and gumnuts you've picked up on your walks with gold or silver spray paint and scatter them around your house. Pile them into glass bowls or cover trays with foil and pile them onto the trays. Add tartan ribbon bows for an extra touch.

Food

Decorating Christmas cakes Buy a large plastic holly decoration at a discount shop and unravel it into three or four smaller pieces and use to decorate the top of your cake. Pipe on Merry Christmas in icing or buy a tube of Cake Mate gel (one tube will go a long way). Wrap the cake first in baking paper and then with a band of Christmas paper cut the same size. Store in an airtight container.

Christmas dinner

Christmas dinner is just one meal during the year and yet, if we let it, this one meal can cost the equivalent of a week's grocery budget. Now, don't get me wrong, I love Christmas, I love Christmas Day and I love having the whole family together; I just don't think it has to be hideously expensive. We make our Christmas dinner special in the way we set the table, serve the food and, of course, share it with family and friends. I use my best china, cutlery and linen and decorate the table with a Christmas tree centrepiece, bon bons and candles. Having strong English and Scottish roots, we enjoy a traditional roast dinner—despite the fact that it can be a blazing 40°C outside! I've done the sums and walked the supermarket aisles to check the prices, and this year our Christmas dinner for six will come in at under $50—and that includes treats and nibbles. There will be dips and savoury biscuits, roast chicken and lovely vegetables, followed by my version of Ice-cream Christmas Pudding. We'll be eating with people we like, the table will look lovely, we'll have food we all like and best of all we'll have spent less than we would on lunch for two at a restaurant!

Family Christmas Activities

While the traditional Christmas lunch or dinner is still an Australian favourite, more and more families are choosing child-friendly activities for Christmas Day. We have heaps of fun-filled low-cost or no-cost ideas. Some favourites are:

The zoo Many zoos are open on Christmas Day.

The local river or stream Find a shady riverbank in an area with slow-flowing water that is not too deep so the children can wade and play. Always keep an eye on the children and ensure they follow safe water practices.

The beach or bay Remember to slip, slop and slap and take some shade for young children and plenty of water.

Local playgrounds or barbecue areas Have Christmas at a local park, throw a prawn on the barbie and let the kids run around and have fun.

> **Christmas is all about the children. After the hype and rush before Christmas, some open space and a chance to run and play is just what the children need.**

Parties

The Best Birthdays

Every year it seems that birthday parties get bigger, more complicated and more expensive. Every parent loves to see their children celebrating their birthdays with their friends and family. It is all too easy for the cost of these parties to get entirely out of hand very quickly. Holding a birthday party doesn't have to be so expensive that you need to take out a second mortgage. You can have a great party, with fabulous decorations, for just a few dollars. Here are some of the things we do to keep our parties within budget.

Try starting the day off with a surprise for the birthday child (or grown-up). Once the birthday child is asleep the night before the big day, blow up a bunch of balloons and tie them to the end of their bed or to a doorhandle. Make a Happy Birthday banner and hang this up where they'll see it when they wake up.

You could also give them a special birthday breakfast. Try pink pancakes for a girl, blue for a boy. The pancake mixture can be made before you go to bed and left in the fridge overnight, ready to cook in the morning.

Planning

Some birthday parties are so grand they almost rival a coronation. They are expensive, time-consuming and stressful to organise and host. In reality, kids are still kids. When all is said and done they want a party that they can share with their friends that is full of good food, games and lots of laughter. Having your child's birthday party at home doesn't have to be hard work. A little planning can make it a breeze. If your child is old enough to know what a birthday party is, then they are old enough to help with the planning. Generally, as long as you give kids options, they are willing to negotiate. If you set a budget with them up front, the party becomes an opportunity for them to learn how to budget—and have fun while they are doing it. Getting the birthday child involved makes the event even more special to them and it ensures that you'll give them what they want. After all, it is their big day.

Themes

Create a fun theme for your child's party. Look through books and magazines for inspiration and let the birthday child choose. To make things a little easier for you, offer two or three choices: a favourite colour, sport, movie, toy or game. Having a theme makes the party easier to plan—it determines the type of cake, decorations, games and food you have. If you decide on a theme birthday cake, it is a good idea to choose early in the piece—just so you can make sure you can make it or buy one for a reasonable price. Some of our favourite themes are:

- Fairy Party
- Barbie Party
- Beach Party
- Popstar Party
- Pirate Party
- Zoo Party
- Football Party

Invitations

Make the party invitations fun and be sure to include all the information that your guests need to know: the date, time (start and finish), birthday person's name, party location and party theme. There are great ways to do this for very little cost. The cheapest way is to make your own invitations. Be creative and work with your children to make them from scratch. Use cardboard, wallpaper scraps, index cards or poster board as a base and add stickers, draw pictures or cut out pictures from wrapping paper, and sprinkle over glitter. Or you can use your computer to print invitations—there are plenty of free programs you can use to create stylish invitations.

Take a look at the discount stores, too, you will find notepad invitations and cards for a couple of dollars. There are various designs for boys and girls so keep your eyes open.

You can be really frugal and send an e-card as an invitation. Make the invitations to suit your theme and if it is to be a costume party, don't forget to mention this on the invitation.

Food

Children at parties are often so busy that they don't want to stop and eat. Having a selection of hot and cold finger foods will be easier for you and your guests and you'll have less waste, too. Instead of making and serving lots of sweets, make the birthday cake the dessert part of the feast. Ensure that everyone gets a piece of birthday cake, so that you won't have cake left over.

Your birthday feast can be delicious and tempting without consisting mainly of junk food. It is possible to have healthy party food that still looks like party food.

Here are some great party ideas:

- Party pies
- Mini sausage rolls
- Cheese and leek balls
- Fairy bread
- French onion dip
- Carrot and celery sticks
- Chips
- Popcorn
- Punch
- Ice-cream cones
- Birthday cake

Drinks

Parents will be grateful if you avoid lots of coloured soft drinks and cordials. Punch is an ideal alternative. Name the punch to suit the party theme; for example, a Pirate Party could have Precious Gem Punch, or a Fairy Party could have Fairy Nectar.

Punch

3 litres tropical fruit juice

1 x 1.25 ml bottle dry ginger ale

1 x 1.25 ml bottle lemonade

1 cup fruit-cup-flavoured cordial

Combine ingredients in a large bowl, pour into 2-litre cordial bottles and store in the fridge. To serve, pour into a large bowl and float ice cubes on top.

Partyware

Visit discount party stores or go online and see what you can find. Plan ahead so that you don't have to buy at full price.

I encourage my kids to plan their birthday themes at least two months ahead of the event so I can begin my shopping early. I have often found discount party stores that are clearing out old stock. When they are doing this you can find some really great bargains. If your kids are like mine, they have a lot of different interests so don't be afraid to mix and match their favourite themes. One year we had a Fairy party with purple napkins, Barbie plates and cups and a Hickory Dickory Dock birthday cake. I bought them all for less than 50 per cent of their normal prices. My daughter and her friends loved it.

Disposable accessories can be expensive, so consider stocking up on inexpensive brightly coloured plastic plates and cups for kids that you can use once the party is over. Add some flair by using matching or contrasting coloured napkins, napkin rings and party favours.

Have a party box

Put together a party box so that you always have the essentials on hand. Include birthday banners, balloons, candles and napkins and anything else that takes your fancy. Each year add any reusable or unused party decorations, plates, utensils, cups etc. Carefully remove tape, tacks and staples from decorations, fold, roll, or tie them up and pack them away. Save what you can of wrapping paper and tissue paper, too. You can iron out the wrinkles for the next use. Cut away tears and gobs of tape, and store in an envelope or folder. Rather than trying to reuse the paper, keep it for your children to use for cut-outs, pictures, projects and other craft activities.

In my party box I have enough cups, plates, bowls and cutlery for twenty-five people. They are all different colours—blue, pink, green and yellow— and were incredibly cheap, six pieces for $2 from a discount store. I have picked up large plastic serving platters and bowls for $2 a piece and they are in the party box too. As they are made of fairly sturdy plastic, they will last for years. I also add balloons, streamers, party favours, lolly bags, etc. that I buy on sale throughout the year. This helps keep the costs down, and takes a lot of the last-minute stress out of planning.

Decorations

Let your children create the ultimate party decorations. Little hands, and happy hearts, will enthusiastically help you bring the party to life. If you would rather buy them yourself, think about buying plain coloured or messaged streamers, banners and so on that can be reused. For example, you can pick up a 50-cent Happy Birthday banner that can be reused many times. Balloons and coloured streamers are a quick and effective way to decorate. A pretty table centrepiece can be made by gathering five small balloons into a bunch. Tie them to a stick, sit the stick in a small jar of sand and tie some curling ribbon around the jar.

Tablecloths provide an opportunity to be creative.

Memento tablecloth Buy some white linen/cotton or use a single bed sheet for the tablecloth. Place coloured permanent markers on the table and encourage the children to write and draw on the tablecloth. When the party is over, launder as usual and fold or roll up gently and tie with a ribbon. This can be a keepsake for your child.

Theme tablecloth Try using a roll of birthday wrapping paper, pretty fabric, a sheet, a large curtain or a clear plastic shower curtain that works with your party theme.

Games

Traditional party games such as musical chairs, pin the tail on the donkey, pass the parcel and a treasure hunt can be adapted to suit just about any theme. For prizes you can use treats that relate to the theme that you have made or bought very cheaply—they don't have to be extravagant. For a sport party you could have gold medals on ribbons as prizes; a fairy party could have glycerine soaps in fairy shapes; a pirate party could have tiny treasure chests filled with chocolate money. Pencils, fancy sharpeners, little cars and stickers also make good prizes.

Loot and lolly bags

You can choose to make up old-fashioned lolly bags with just lollies and balloons or make up loot bags with lollies, balloons and small party favours. The bags can be simple sandwich bags, more elaborately decorated and themed plastic bags or you can personalise brown paper lunch bags for each child. Again, you are limited only by your imagination. A great idea is to use party hats as loot bags—the kids will probably not wear them anyway. Line each hat with a paper napkin and top with lollies. The elastic acts as a handle and each guest will have something to take home that they can play with later.

What you put into your bags is determined by the age of the guests. Older children may prefer fewer lollies and more trinkets. Girls like fancy soaps, nail polishes, pencils, sharpeners and hair accessories. Boys like super balls, foam gliders, cars, plastic bugs, etc.

Try matching the contents of the bags to the theme so that it carries through to the end of the party.

Saying goodbye

Two to 2½ hours is more than enough for a birthday party. The last thing you want is overexcited, overtired guests getting emotional. Make sure you put an end time on your invitations and as each child is dropped off remind parents of the pick-up time. When it's time to go, have the birthday child hand out the lolly bags and say thank you and goodbye to each guest and their parents as they leave.

Part 3:

CHEAPSKATE
success stories

Barry and Rachael

Young Family

While some might jest at the things that Cheapskates do to save money, the simple facts and figures clearly show that it is the **only** smart way to live. Irrespective of how much income you make, if you have any debt—mortgage, credit card or personal loans—you need to have these paid off as soon as possible. Being a Cheapskate enables you to do that.

Take a look at this family whose real identity we'll conceal for obvious reasons. Let's call them the Simmonds family: husband Barry, wife Rachael and two young boys, Sam and Jake, under five years of age. Barry brings home a good wage—he makes $75,000 per year—and Rachael looks after the children. They live in Sydney, have a mortgage of $350,000, credit card debts of $3000 and a car loan of $9000. Interest rate rises, increased petrol costs—Barry drives 45 minutes to and from work daily—and increasing food costs had hurt the family and when we met they were slipping further and further into debt.

The Simmonds family decided their way to a stress-free life was to reduce their debt and they came to Cheapskates looking for answers. They were seriously frightened that they could lose their house because their debt was steadily rising. Rather than letting it spiral out of control, they decided to take action.

To become Cheapskates, Barry and Rachael had to commit to changing five of their shopping, buying and spending habits. They agreed to:

1. Take lunch to work
2. Change detergents and washing powders for homemade, more environmentally friendly versions
3. No unnecessary shopping
4. Shop fortnightly rather than weekly
5. Have takeaway food once a week rather than three times a week

1 Take lunch to work

In the past Barry spent:

- $2.50 for a coffee on the way to work
- At least $6 on a sandwich (in winter he often had pasta or a hot meal for $9)
- $3 on a drink
- $2.20 on an afternoon snack

  Total amount spent $12.30
  Barry has now committed to:

- Coffee—getting up 5 minutes earlier each day and making coffee at home using their espresso machine. Buying expensive ground coffee and milk works out to a cost of 50 cents per cup. This is a saving of $2 per day
- Lunch—taking a homemade sandwich or leftover meal from home. Cost $2, which is a saving of at least $4 per day
- Drink—Rachael buys soft drink multi-packs from the supermarket. The usual price is 53 cents per can, though Rachael has found she can get them on sale for as low as 45 cents per can, which is a saving of $2.50 per day

- Afternoon snack—is also supermarket-bought for $1.60. Rachael often buys packets or chooses the ones on sale and gets them for $1 per bar, which is a saving of 60 cents per day
- Total saving $8.60 per day. Rachael reports she buys on sale and often saves closer to $9 per day.

Total saving $1978 (46 weeks x 5 days x $8.60) a year!

2 Change detergents and washing powders

With two young boys Rachael washes daily. She used a laundry powder concentrate that cost $6.46 per packet. She bought one box every two weeks, which amounted to a total yearly cost of $167.96. Now, Rachael uses our washing powder and it costs her 0.03 cents per load with a total yearly cost of just $10.95. That's a saving of $157.01 per year.

Rachael has switched from using commercial kitchen cleaners, bathroom sprays, detergents, laundry cleaners and floor cleaners to white vinegar and bicarb soda. Her yearly cost for detergents and other cleaners was over $300. (She was buying two new cleaning products a week with the average product costing $5.95. This amounted to $618.80 a year. Rachael admitted that she often fell for the advertising on TV.) Rachael now buys 2 litres of white vinegar for $1.47 and a 1-kilogram packet of bicarb soda for $2.87.

Rachael cleans daily and the vinegar lasts for two weeks, so this costs $41.16 a year. The bicarb lasts for six months, so this has a total cost of $5.74 a year. Rachael set about using up all the old products she had left and in the next twelve months spent a total of $46.90 on cleaning products.

Total saving $571.90 a year!

3 No unnecessary shopping

Rachael and Barry decided that they could both give up buying new clothes for themselves and fishing rods and knick-knacks for the next twelve months while they worked to get ahead. The credit card statements revealed they had spent $3422 on such things in the last twelve months. By putting a freeze on this spending for one year they automatically saved that amount of money.

Total saving $3422 a year!

4 Fortnightly shopping

Barry and Rachael agreed that it was really difficult to go shopping and not walk out with extra items. One of the simplest ways to reduce overspending is to shop less and when shopping to limit the amount of time spent in the shops. This was hard, as they both spent a lot of time shopping. Instead, they committed to spending Saturday mornings at the park with the children. The boys love it and even in winter they found they had fun. If it was raining they played inside the house. Saturday mornings became the children's time and the shopping became less and less attractive, so now Rachael makes a quick run to the shops and is home within the hour. They have cut their grocery bill from $250 per week to just $250 per fortnight. In other words they halved the grocery bill.

Some of this saving came from changing cleaning products; other savings came from choosing fresh food. Rachael now bakes with the boys each week rather than buying biscuits and she watches the prices and looks for sales to save wherever possible.

Though she now has the added expense of buying Barry's lunch and snacks within the grocery budget, they eat at home more and are living very well for $250 per fortnight.

Total saving $3000 per year!

5 Have takeaway food once a week

Rachael was often tired after the hectic days with the children and Barry would grab takeaway on the way home. The family was eating an average of 156 takeaway meals a year at an average cost of $30 per meal! This means that their total takeaway food bill was around $4680 per year.

Barry and Rachael reduced fast food meals to once a week, which reduced the cost to $1560 per year.

Total saving $3120 per year!

Total savings

Lunch	$2064
Cleaning	$571.90
Unnecessary shopping	$3422
Fortnightly shopping	$3000
Fast food	$3120
Total	**$12,177.90**

Make your savings go further

Let's look at Barry and Rachael's loans. The interest rate on the credit card was nearly 18 per cent, the car loan 11 per cent and the mortgage 7.5 per cent.

The strategy

For many of us it is hard to budget and to see savings. While you are putting in this effort, you want to see results. For the first three months Barry and Rachael took out the normal amount of money, but for each little bit they saved, they paid themselves. In other words, they had a tin (in a secret hiding spot) and each day that Barry saved money on lunch he was able to add $8.60 to the tin. Likewise, when Rachael shopped fortnightly and spent only $250, she put the $250 she'd saved in the tin. And so on and so on … While this might sound silly, they then went to the bank each fortnight and put this money from the tin into paying off their credit card. As you can imagine, the credit card bill was gone within a few short months.

Barry and Rachael said, 'It was like being children again. Each week, we made a special time to count our savings up and we checked our statement to see it going down. We celebrated with the boys when it was zero—though not outside our budget. We had a family "no credit card bill" barbecue at the park. The boys, especially our eldest boy, were eager to understand what we had done that we were so excited about, so hopefully he can learn from our mistake.'

Twelve months on, Barry and Rachael have continued to pay off the house loan at the normal amount but have now channelled every other cent into the car loan, which is already halved in size.

They have taken on board some other cost savings and now save nearly $20,000. Through their calculations they will be able to start to increase their house repayments within six months and by paying the extra off the loan will reduce the loan to nine years, saving them over $100,000 in interest charges.

Being Cheapskates has changed Barry and Rachael forever. Rather than coping with huge debts that were overwhelming them, they have created a financial plan to which they are committed. They are in control and feel as though they have a secure future: they are putting money away for the children's education, yearly holidays and their retirement. They spend more time in the sunshine with their boys and feel fitter and healthier because of the increased exercise and better food they are eating.

Jack and Emily

Retirees

When Jack and Emily came to Cheapskates for help they had been happily married for over thirty years. Jack had just retired and they were finding it difficult to make ends meet. They found that their superannuation was inadequate and the retirement they had dreamed about was fast becoming a nightmare. Their pension was nowhere near enough to cover their bills and give them the lifestyle they had enjoyed while Jack worked. In the first eight months of retirement they had already begun to rack up credit card debts. Thankfully they had paid off their home and car, but there were still monthly bills for insurance, registration, utilities and food. They wanted to go north for the winter each year, although they couldn't see how they could afford this.

Eighteen months later, Jack and Emily are now planning their first holiday north. While life has changed for them, they are in control of their bills, have paid off the credit card and have saved enough for a holiday without going into debt.

Make your savings go further

Jack and Emily were no strangers to saving: when first married they had done it tough buying a house and raising three children. Understandably, they did not want to go back to this kind of struggle in their retirement. But we know that being a Cheapskate is not about living a miserable life. Instead it is about finding ways to save on everyday bills, so that our money can be used for the important things in our lives.

Jack and Emily took some time to scour through the thousands of tips on the Cheapskate website and Emily came back very excited. 'There are a lot of simple things that we can do that will decrease our costs. Most of them are small things, but adding them all together will certainly help us to save.'

The strategy
Some of the things that Jack and Emily chose to do to save money included:

1 Change cleaning products
They began to use our homemade versions.
   Total saving about $200 per year!

2 Eat at home
Over the years they had begun to eat out at restaurants twice a week. They spent $60 per meal on average and were shocked when they realised this was costing them $6240 per year. Not surprisingly, they reduced their restaurant meals to once a fortnight. They calculated the cost for the fortnightly restaurant meal would be $1560.
   Total saving $4680!

3 Make lunch
They decided that rather than buying lunch when out shopping, they would eat at home. Lunch and coffee cost $20, whereas lunch at home cost about $5. Where they were spending $1040 eating out, eating at home would cost them $260.
   Total saving $780!

4 Stop buying clothes

Jack and Emily decided that they had enough clothes. Upon retiring they had splurged on some new casual clothes and had an overflowing wardrobe. They committed to buying only essential clothes from now on. They set a yearly budget of $400.

Total saving at least $1000!

5 Grandchildren's presents

Jack and Emily loved their five grandchildren. They often spent hundreds of dollars on Christmas and birthday presents. They decided that it was time to be realistic. They set themselves a budget of $50 per grandchild for Christmas and the same for birthdays and bought presents in the sales. This helped to increase the value of the present and allowed them to save some additional money. From spending over $1000 per year, they budgeted on spending $500.

Total saving $500!

6 Children's presents

While sorting out saving for the grandchildren, Jack and Emily took the plunge and talked to their children. They explained that they wanted to save money for their trip and asked the children if they would mind if for their Christmas and birthdays they gave them small, thoughtful, inexpensive gifts. Their children were all doing well and encouraged them not to spend any money at all on them—rather they encouraged them to save for their trip. They decided to spend $20 on each occasion—a total of $120. Jack and Emily said they got very good at shopping for good-value items for their children and grandchildren. Often they bought presents with a normal ticket price of double what they ended up paying. They asked for discounts, looked out for sales, asked for seniors' discounts and bought multiple items to reduce the costs.

Total saving $180!

7 Petrol

Jack and Emily were eligible for a card that enabled them to travel by train for $2 a day within Melbourne because they are pensioners. Rather than driving to town they started to catch the train. Likewise, they found the tram a fun way to travel with the grandchildren. They walked more, multi-tasked journeys, started to catch the bus to visit friends or get around and chose not to drive, saving them as much as $20 per week in petrol. This money would pay for their fuel costs to drive to Queensland for their holiday.

Total saving $900!

8 Bonus activities

Jack and Emily decided to join Probus. While there was a joining fee and they went out with the group once a month for lunch, they found it was a great social network. They shared their plans with their new-found friends within the group. They soon had an active life where, instead of going out to restaurants, they had card nights and dinner parties at home where they could control the costs.

Total savings

Cleaning $200
  Restaurants $4680
  Lunch $780

Clothes $1000
Grandchildren's presents $500
Children's presents $180
Petrol $900
Total $8240

Jack and Emily said that life was action-packed and fun, even though they watched their costs. They paid off the credit card debt and had a great holiday in Queensland. The funny thing they found was that their life was something they enjoyed, though not what they had imagined, 'Retirement,' they said 'is one of the best times in our life.'

Samantha

Corporate Executive

Samantha is not the sort of person you imagine would become a Cheapskate. A successful HR executive, Samantha's recent promotion had increased her salary to over $100,000 per year. She thoroughly enjoyed her new position and the lifestyle it afforded her. In anyone's terms, Samantha was on a good deal. She had a hectic schedule packed with social events, travel and plenty of shopping at all the best designer stores. Samantha had dinner parties with guests enjoying the spectacular views from her new Dockland apartment. In an extravagant moment, she had lashed out and bought a new BMW convertible. While life seemed to be terrific, Samantha had a nagging concern that her personal debt was extremely high, and really, she had very little to show for all the money she had spent.

Reading that she had reached the maximum level on her second credit card one Saturday morning, Samantha decided that she wanted to change her lifestyle. She took a pen and tallied her debts: nearly $35,000 in credit cards, attracting a staggering 17.5 per cent interest, a personal loan on the car of $52,000, with interest rates of 11 per cent, and rent payments of $350 per week. Samantha said she felt ill when she realised what she had done. The money had gone to her head. She was overspending, living beyond her means and heading for trouble.

Samantha looked through her credit card statements at how much she spent on restaurants, drinks, clothes, shoes, insurance, cash advances, etc., etc ... She went searching on the internet for a program to help her change her life. Her research led her to Cheapskates and while she admitted she did not like being called a Cheapskate, she got the message that she could have a great lifestyle, pay off her debts and begin to save for her future. Samantha began by reading the thousands of ways she could save money. She made an extensive list then timetabled when and how she would begin her new life.

Samantha looked through the last six months of credit card bills. With a calculator she quickly found she was averaging the following costs:

1. Clothes, casual, work and eveningwear, and shoes over $2000 per month ($24,000)
2. Dinner parties, food and alcohol, an average of $500 per month ($6000)
3. Restaurants $650 per month ($7800)
4. Nightclubs $150 per week ($7800)
5. Weekends away and holidays average of $1250 per month ($15,000)
6. Lunch $20 per day ($5000)
7. Café lattes $6 per day ($2190)
8. Lottery tickets $20 per week ($1040)
9. Car detailing $50 per fortnight ($1300)
10. Gifts and presents $200 per month, Christmas $3000 ($5400)
11. Cleaner $60 per week ($3120)
12. Magazines $50 per month ($600)
13. CDs $120 per month ($1440)

Grand (and horrifying) total $80,690

Make your savings go further

Samantha was shocked. Now she knew why she was racking up the debt. Last year's bonus of $9000 had vanished and now she had all this debt. She said she couldn't see the view—her eyes welled up and for the first time she regretted the beautiful apartment of which she had been so proud.

The strategy

Samantha began immediately. She decided there were things on her list that she wasn't happy with. If she halved every cost on the list, she would have the money to pay off her credit card in one year, and have a little extra to begin a savings plan. So that is want she did. She had the cleaner come fortnightly, the car was detailed every month, she cut back to one café latte and she began to have a sandwich and juice for lunch.

Samantha cut out the gambling and decided that she needed only one magazine a week and two CDs per month. She also decided that the amount she spent on clothes and shoes was insane. Yes, she loved shopping; however, a healthy share portfolio would be a better investment.

Two years on and Samantha is extremely proud to be a Cheapskate. She still has the credit cards and uses them rather than carrying cash; however, they are paid off every month without fail. She is one year ahead on her car loan and has bought $8000 in shares. Samantha found that the more she saw her debt reducing, the faster she wanted it gone. She found there were plenty of cost-effective ways to have fun.

Samantha told us that she now spends less than one-quarter of the money on the items on the list. She said the amazing part was that she still had a fantastic lifestyle. As she began to change, she developed new friendships that encouraged and supported her new lifestyle. They now take advantage of the wonderful outdoor locations around the Docklands, going bike riding along the bay foreshore and enjoying the beach and parklands. Samantha said that they had wonderful 'cuisine picnics', they visited wineries in the Yarra Valley, drove down to the peninsula and above all laughed a lot.

Michael and Sarah

Young Couple

Michael completed his carpentry apprenticeship and had a salary of $35,000 in his final year. He was fortunate to pick up a contract on a large construction site in Brisbane and added a few thousand to his pay packet. Michael is no different to most young men. He loves his car, enjoys a drink with the lads and likes clubbing on the weekends. Michael had recently met the love of his life and was enjoying all the attention of a new romance. Michael and his partner Sarah decided to move in together and like most young people gave the finances limited thought.

Now ten months on, Michael and Sarah had maxed out credit cards, the rent was due, he was one repayment behind on his car and he was not feeling so happy. Michael had not realised how much it cost to live in a flat. Rent was $200 per week, and then there were all the utility bills. Not having the rent money meant Michael had to go home and ask Mum and Dad for another loan. This time, they said they wanted to have a talk before handing over the money. During this talk they made Michael and Sarah write down all their debts. It was most uncomfortable. Michael's list was depressing:

1. Car loan $19,500, with an interest rate of 13.5 per cent
2. First credit card, $11,000
3. Second credit card $2500
4. Rent due $200
5. Loans from Mum and Dad $3000

6. Interest-free loans that were about to be due: $800 on a fridge, $2000 on furniture and $900 on a barbecue and outdoor furniture.

Michael said that he felt like the biggest loser. He kept arguing that he had to buy this stuff. His Mum and Dad were not criticising him, just pointing out that now he must find a way to pay for it all.

Michael began to think seriously about his situation and he realised that he and Sarah were going to have to make some changes. Sarah's finances were just as bad, and if they wanted to stay together and not fight all the time, they had to take action. Michael began to look at his main expenses:

Payment on credit cards

Michael looked at his statements. He always paid the minimum amount so each month he was paying 17.5 per cent interest on each card.

Food

Michael knew he spent a lot on food, but as he said, he worked hard and he was not overweight, in fact, the family joked that he had hollow legs.

- Breakfast—he grabs something to eat from the local fast food options each morning. Usually costing him $8-10
- Morning tea—a pie and soft drink $6
- Lunch—Michael liked to have a steak sandwich or burger with the lot, flavoured milk, cake or muffin $10
- Afternoon—an energy drink or soft drink with a chocolate bar $5

- Dinner—At home or takeaway—if takeaway food, Michael and Sarah usually had pizza ($20), Chinese ($40), pasta or noodles ($28), fish and chips ($20)
- Restaurants/cafes usually three nights per week $50.

Total amount spent $295 per week. That was a massive investment of $15,340 per year.

Make your savings go further

The strategy

Michael and Sarah talked about how they could get organised, take some meals from home to save some money and buy drinks and chocolate bars from the supermarket. This would reduce Michael's daily food costs by 40 per cent. Sarah agreed to help Michael make tasty sandwiches and rolls. Michael bought two thermal lunchboxes (breakfast/morning tea in one, lunch in the other).

Michael and Sarah decided that they could cut down costs further if they started to cook at home. To make it fun, Sarah decided to do a Thai cooking class that she had always wanted to do and Michael confessed he would like to try some Jamie Oliver recipes. They calculated they could eat terrific food and still cut their food bill in half.

Sarah could cut down on monthly shopping sprees. Sarah, like most fashion-conscious twenty-two-year-olds, loves shoes and often spent up to $300 on a new pair. She bought a new outfit every week costing $100–$150. An evening gown she had recently put on her credit card cost $900. Sarah decided that she too had a problem with her credit card and by reducing the amount she spent to $200 per month she could begin to pay off the credit card and still have plenty of new clothes.

Michael and Sarah looked for other ideas to save money. They liked the Cheapskate idea of using natural cleaning products in their apartment, so they started using white vinegar and bicarb soda.

They could reduce their heating and cooling costs, cut down electricity use by turning off appliances and lights—which they felt was doing their part in helping to reduce global warming, too.

Mobile phones cost them $79 per month, so they committed to reduce usage and costs when their current contracts expired.

All these savings would easily total $600–$800 per year and they decided to reward themselves with a long weekend away to Fraser Island.

Twelve months on and Michael and Sarah asked Michael's parents if they could sit down and share their wins with them. Proudly they showed how they had paid a lot off their credit cards. Michael pulled out the receipts showing he had paid off the interest-free loans for the furniture and was well on the way to paying off the fridge and barbecue. He realised he was actually paying 32 per cent interest and was suitably unimpressed with the sales gimmicks major retailers used.

Michael and Sarah found that they enjoyed the time they spent together creating gourmet meals. In fact, when they invited friends around to share meals, they found their friends were envious of their relationship and ability to save money.

They quickly found that alcohol, though not originally something they had added to their list, was a major expense. When they went out they were being charged $6–$8 per drink and even at home they often went through $80–$90 in wine and beer when they were entertaining. They told their friends to BYO alcohol, a further saving of over $100 per week.

Michael and Sarah were well on the way to clearing their debts, they spent quality time together and found that they had built a strong bond. Sure Michael still loved his car and Sarah loved to go out with her friends, but they realised they had similar goals and dreams too. In fact, they told Michael's parents that they were going to continue to save for the next three years so that they could have a good deposit for their first house when they get married.

Conclusion

Being a Cheapskate is not just about saving money; misers do that. Cheapskates realise that it is about spending more time with the people you care about and planning a safe and secure future.

At Cheapskates we wish you well with your plans. Please visit our website at:

www.cheapskates.com.au/cheapskatesway

A—Budget Planner

(1) INCOME		WEEKLY/FORTNIGHTLY/MONTHLY	
Salary (1)		Centrelink Pension/Benefit (1)	
Salary (2)		Centrelink Pension/Benefit (2)	
Child Support		Family Payment	
Board/Rent			
Investments			
Total A		**Total B**	
		Total A & B	
(2) EXPENDITURE		FIXED PAYMENTS	
Rent/Mortgage		Car Registration	
Rates		Car Insurance	
Electricity/Gas		House Insurance	
Phone		Contents Insurance	
Mobile Phone		Medical Insurance	
Day Care		School Fees	
Superannuation – personal		Other	
Total C		**Total D**	
		Total C & D	

(3) EXPENDITURE		FLEXIBLE PAYMENTS		
Petrol		Birthday/Christmas/Gifts		
Fares		Sports/Hobbies		
Food		Pets		
Alcohol/Cigarettes		Papers/Magazines		
Clothing/Shoes		Subscription/Membership		
Entertainment		Donation		
Property Maintenance		Holidays		
School Sports/Excursions		Personal – Hairdresser		
Total E		Total F		
		Total E&F		
(4) CREDITORS				
1.		4.		
2.		5.		
3.		6.		
		Combined Total Payments		
		Total Expenses	2	
			3	
			4	
Total Income (1)		Total Expenditure	$	
		Surplus/Deficit	$	

B—A Sample Price Book page

Use this sample page to start your price book. A simple, spiral notebook with about 50 pages will get you started.

	Item			
Date	Store	Size	Unit price	Price

C—Daily Time Block Chart

	Routine Chores/Errands	Special Chores/Errands	Phone Calls/Emails
9:00am–10:00am			
10:00am–11:00am			
11:00am–12:00pm			
12:00pm–1:00pm			
1:00pm–2:00pm			
2:00pm–3:00pm			
3:00pm–4:00pm			
4:00pm–5:00pm			

D—Credit Counselling Services

Australian Capital Territory
- Care Financial Counselling Service
  02 6257 1788

New South Wales
- NSW Financial Counsellors Association
  0500 888 079
  www.financialcounsellors.asn.au
- CreditLine Helpline
  1800 808 488
- Credit Line Financial Counselling
  Services
  www.wesleymission.org.au/
  centres/creditline/counselling.asp

Northern Territory
- Anglicare Northern Territory
  Financial Counselling Service
  08 8948 2700 or 08 8985 0000

Queensland
- Financial Counselling Association
  of Queensland
  07 332 13192

South Australia
- Uniting Care Wesley
  08 8202 5111
- The South Australia Financial
  Counselling Association's website lists
  financial counsellors in South Australia
  www.users.bigpond.com/safca/

Tasmania
- Anglicare Financial Counselling Service
  03 6234 3510 or 1800 243 232
- Consumer Credit Solicitor at Hobart
  Community Legal Service
  03 6223 2500 or 1800 232 500

Victoria
- Financial and Consumer Rights Council
  03 966 32000
- Consumer Affairs Victoria
  1300 55 8181
- Financial and Consumer Rights Council
  lists all financial counsellors in Victoria
  http://avoca.vicnet.net.au/~fcrc/

Western Australia
- Consumer Credit Legal Service
  08 9481 7665
- Financial Counsellor's
  Association of WA
  08 9325 1617

Index